6733
(8) X

656

D0345939

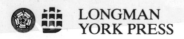

LONGMAN
YORK PRESS

YORK PRESS
Immeuble Esseily, Place Riad Solh, Beirut

LONGMAN GROUP UK LIMITED
Longman House, Burnt Mill, Harlow,
Essex CM20 2JE, England
Associated companies, branches and representatives
throughout the world

First published 1982
Fifth impression 1992

ISBN 0-582-78288-0

Printed in Hong Kong
WLEE/05

Contents

Contents

Part 1

Introduction

The Augustan age of English literature

In 27BC, when Julius Caesar's nephew, Octavius (63BC–AD14) had mastered his rivals and made himself sole ruler of Rome and its empire, he took the name Augustus, denoting his intention to rule in peace and prosperity, which he did for forty years. During this time of political stability, the literary arts flourished. Augustus himself encouraged both Virgil and Horace.

When Charles II returned to England from France in 1660, after the Civil War and the rule of Oliver Cromwell, the poet John Dryden (1631–1700) hailed him as an English Augustus, destined to restore the country to peace and to foster the arts. Charles did indeed encourage literature, especially the theatre, and he brought with him from France standards of taste based on what were thought to be classical principles, derived from the Greek philosopher Aristotle (384–322BC) and the Roman poet Horace (65–8BC). English writers consciously set out to emulate the Augustan age of Roman literature.

The result is a period of literature dedicated to clarity, balance and the classical tradition. By the first was meant a plainness of meaning which avoided obscure wit, complicated word-play or references to facts or ideas not readily understood by the ordinary reader. By the second was meant a tone of writing which avoided extremes of emotion and a point of view which avoided extremes of opinion. By the last was meant a constant and conscious attention to classical literature, that is, the literature of ancient Greece and Rome, as a model and source of ideas, phrases and allusions. But the imitation of the classics was not to be merely literary. It was meant also to be moral. Literature was to recreate the values of duty, piety, justice and integrity which were thought to be the glory of Roman civilisation and its foundation.

John Dryden was the first great Augustan writer in English literature. Alexander Pope (1688–1744) was the second, and together with Jonathan Swift (1667–1745) and Joseph Addison (1672–1759) he so dominated his period that his lifetime is often described as the Augustan age in English literature. But both Samuel Johnson (1709–84) and Henry Fielding (1707–54) have Augustan qualities and carry the ideal beyond the middle of the century.

There is, however, a paradox about Augustanism in England. Most of its major exponents were writers in opposition to the state, driven to attack the government, not celebrate it. Almost all the Augustans were satirists, opposed to the social changes of their England. The lofty ideal they proclaimed never became manifest in reality. It remained the standard by which they condemned their age, but the age went on regardless. No wonder, then, if behind the calm, neoclassical surface of Augustan literature strong emotions are to be found, and that murky, irascible feelings make works such as Pope's *Dunciad* (1743) or Swift's *Gulliver's Travels* (1726) less classical, more complex and more interesting than any generalisation about the Age of Reason would allow.

Pope's life

Alexander Pope's life was uneventful. He was born in London on 21 May 1688. About twelve years later the family moved to Windsor Forest and at about this time Pope began to show signs of poetic talent. Several older friends of the family encouraged him and he became known in London literary circles. By his twenty-fifth year he was acquainted with Swift, Addison, John Gay (1685–1732) and a number of noblemen and politicians. In 1715 his translation of Homer began to appear. By its success Pope made enough money to achieve financial security. In 1716 he moved to Chiswick, near London, and two years later finally settled at Twickenham, a few miles up-river from the capital. Here he embellished his house and gardens and entertained his many friends. He returned those visits in several tours of some of the great country houses of southern England. He never travelled much further than Bath, and never left England. He did not marry. He died on 30 May 1744.

Pope's literary career

As a boy, Pope read widely in several languages, teaching himself as he read. His first poems were imitations of his favourite poets. Almost from the start he strove for what he called correctness, that is, technical perfection, elegance of expression and sound morality. At the age of twelve he was taken to London to see John Dryden, the greatest poet of the preceding age. This symbolic act confirmed Pope in his vocation. He further linked himself to the traditional line of English poetry by his friendship with Dryden's friends, including William Congreve (1670–1729) and William Wycherley (1640–1716). In 1709 he published his first work, *Pastorals*, charming, artificial poems about the countryside, neo-classical in style. Two years later appeared *An Essay on Criticism*, modelled on Horace's poem *Ars Poetica*, a discussion of poetry and drama of c.20BC. Pope's poem was praised by Addison in his influential magazine *The Spectator*, but attacked by the critic John Dennis. Pope formed a literary society, the Scriblerus Club, with Swift, Gray, Thomas Parnell (1679–1718) and John Arbuthnot (1667–1735), and together they produced a series of works, pamphlets and periodical papers of a satirical nature. At the same time Pope began translating into English verse the epic poems of Homer (ninth century BC) the great Greek poet (Dryden had translated the *Aeneid*, the epic poem by the great Roman poet Virgil (70–19BC)). In 1717 he published a collected edition of his works, containing the full version of *The Rape of the Lock*, *Eloisa to Abelard* and *Elegy to the Memory of an Unfortunate Lady*, as well as his earlier poems. This volume established Pope as the greatest English poet of his time.

In 1720 he completed his translation of Homer's *Iliad* and began work on his *Odyssey*. In translating the latter he was assisted by two minor poets, William Broome and Elijah Fenton. The work was completed in 1726. The previous year Pope had published an edition of Shakespeare's plays. These literary labours had two consequences. First, Pope produced very little original poetry for about ten years, and second, both the Homer and the Shakespeare involved him in literary squabbles. Pope fell out with Addison because the latter preferred the inferior translation of Homer by Addison's friend, Thomas Tickell (1686–1740); and Pope's unscholarly treatment of Shakespeare provoked Lewis Theobald (pronounced 'Tibbald' 1688–1744) into publishing *Shakespeare Restored* (1726), pointing out Pope's mistakes. In retaliation, Pope put together a satirical mock-epic poem, *The Dunciad*, ridiculing the bad writers, or dunces, of the time, with Theobald as hero of the poem. Pope continued to work on this complex satire for the rest of his life, eventually substituting Colley Cibber (1671–1757), the Poet Laureate, for Theobald as hero and expanding the scope of the satire to include the whole of society, not just writers. *The Dunciad* is the background for the long series of satires, including the *Imitations of Horace*, which Pope published between 1731 and his death.

At the beginning of this period, however, he produced a different kind of work, *An Essay on Man*, a poetical discourse on metaphysics, ethics and human nature. This was to be part of a grand series of philosophical poems. But Pope was deflected from his purpose into satirical and political writings. Even the *Essay on Man* was attacked and Pope's gratitude to William Warburton (1689–1779), who wrote in its defence, led to a friendship with important consequences, for Warburton, an overbearing, ambitious man, dominated the poet's last years. He encumbered Pope with help in revising his poems and after the poet's death became his literary executor. His unreliable edition of Pope's works, burdened with notes displaying Warburton's own prejudices, appeared in 1751 and was taken as authoritative until this century.

The wide range of Pope's work was deliberate. He set out to excel in the recognised kinds of poetry, such as pastoral, epic (if only in translation) and heroic epistle. But the most productive period of his career, between 1730 and 1743, was devoted to satire, and satire which grew in ferocity year by year. Pope's increasing belligerence and bitterness suggest he felt more and more isolated from society. To understand this, we must look at the conditions of his life, his religion, his politics and his health.

Historical background

In the sixteenth century Europe was divided by religious differences among Christians. Many northern states, including England, turned Protestant, rejected the authority of the Pope, head of the Roman Catholic Church, and set up independent, national churches. But the states of central and southern Europe, such as France, Spain and Austria, remained Roman Catholic and often sought to restore the authority of their Church in all Europe. Religious wars disturbed the continent until the beginning of the eighteenth century.

In 1688, James II, a Roman Catholic, was forced to give up the crown of England because of his religion. His daughter Mary and her Protestant husband William, a Dutch prince, were invited by Parliament to rule instead. Laws were passed excluding Roman Catholics from the throne. James died in 1701. As his son, also called James, refused to become a Protestant, and as William and Mary's successor, her sister Anne, had no heir, Parliament decided the throne would pass at her death to the Elector of Hanover, ruler of a small state in Germany.

There were Englishmen, however, who did not approve of this alteration of the laws of succession, and there were politicians who took advantage of this. Henry St John, Viscount Bolingbroke (1678–1751), leader of the Tories, a political faction, knew he had offended the Elector of Hanover by negotiating a secret peace with France in 1713. He and others plotted to call James to the throne on Queen Anne's death. Vigorous action by their political opponents, the Whigs, the other main faction, frustrated the plan. George I (reigned 1714–27), Elector of Hanover and thus founder of the Hanoverian dynasty which, although German, was to rule Great Britain for many years, succeeded to the throne in 1714 and immediately installed the Whigs in power. Some Tory leaders were imprisoned; others, like St John, fled abroad. Tainted with Jacobitism (the word comes from *Jacobus*, the Latin form of 'James'), the Tory party was excluded from office and the Whigs exploited their control of the distribution of state appointments and pensions to consolidate their power for the rest of the century. Several

Jacobite plots and risings merely made the Hanoverian kings all the more distrustful of Tory politicians.

Pope's religion

Pope was a Roman Catholic, which caused him to suffer from the hostility of the Government. Catholics had to pay extra taxes; there were laws to prevent their holding Government offices, owning land or living in London or close to the royal court. It is true that these laws were not very strictly enforced, and were more irksome than punitive, but they are the reason Pope had to make money out of his literary works and live in a rented house outside London. The effect of this persecution was to make Pope proud of his independence. When friends in the Government offered him a secret pension, he refused. As a Roman Catholic he was legally isolated. He saw this as a kind of freedom from dependence on the state.

Yet he was not really strongly Roman Catholic, or even very religious. Although he was much involved with Catholic families in England (*The Rape of the Lock* was intended to settle one of their quarrels), he was not confined to their society. His great friend Swift, for example, was a Protestant clergyman. Pope's religious outlook was tolerant and reasonable, laying stress on what all Christians, indeed what all right-thinking men, could agree upon about God and morality.

Pope's politics

In describing the historical background the names Whig and Tory have been used as though they referred to identifiable political parties, but that is more convenient than true. There was no formal party system at the time and the terms indicate inclinations rather than ideologies. Pope's inclinations were Tory, perhaps even Jacobite; he was a close friend of Bolingbroke and of Francis Atterbury, Bishop of Rochester (1662–1732) (see *Epistle to Arbuthnot*, 140), who was banished for Jacobitism. Pope, as a Roman Catholic, could never have taken a direct part in politics, but his literary talent, like that of Addison and Swift, was valued by politicians for propaganda purposes. In the last years of Queen Anne, when the Tories were in power, Pope had been close to the centre of government and the intrigues of court and parliament. With the fall of the Tories, he was driven into opposition, where he poured lofty scorn in his satires on the corruption of the Whigs and praised the idealism of his friends (who called themselves Patriots, because they swore they put the interests of the country before their own). Pope's politics therefore also isolated him. He was opposed to the Hanoverian kings and their governments; and they were opposed to him.

Pope's health

When he was a boy, Pope was infected by cow's milk with a form of tuberculosis which affected his spine. His growth was stunted so that he was never taller than about four and a half feet, with skinny limbs, and a hunchback. As he grew older, the condition worsened. He suffered headaches and pain and needed special clothing to support his body enough for him to sit and walk. He became more and more dependent on other people for help in all sorts of domestic ways. This physical dependence perhaps explains his proud independence of spirit and his idealisation of the life of detachment pictured by Horace.

Naturally Pope was sensitive about his misshapen body, of which his enemies made cruel fun. But more humiliating must have been the attitude of the opposite sex. The venom of his attacks on Lady Mary Wortley Montagu (1689–1762), a writer and intellectual who was at first Pope's friend, may have been caused by her derision of the tender feelings Pope seems to express at the end of *Eloisa to Abelard* (1717). Martha Blount (1690–1763) proved a more lasting friend, and there was talk of her marrying Pope, though she never did.

Pope's health and appearance must have affected his personality and therefore his works. Hostile critics have often asserted that his twisted body was matched by a twisted mind, full of spite and resentment. Pope was certainly a good hater, and he made many enemies; but he also had many firm friends, upon whom he bestowed the finest poetic praise in English literature. What can be said is that, like his religion and his politics, Pope's health served to isolate him from his society.

A note on the text

Pope took considerable care over the publishing of his poems and revised them for each new edition. He was working on a final edition when he died. Unfortunately, he was then under the influence of Warburton, to whom he entrusted the task of publishing his poetical works after his death. Warburton prevailed on the dying Pope to alter some poems and re-title others. The changes were often minor, but sometimes meant rearranging the lines of poems. This can cause confusion in referring to line numbers. Nevertheless, Warburton's 1751 edition remained influential until 1939, when the Twickenham Edition, under the general editorship of John Butt, published by Methuen, London, began to appear. The six volumes of this edition are now standard, and all students of Pope are indebted to its notes and critical introductions. The particular selection of poems to which the following notes refer is *Selected Poems of Pope*, edited by Philip Brockbank, Hutchinson, London, 1964, fifth impression 1979.

Part 2

Summaries
of SELECTED POEMS BY POPE

Introductory note

Several people and places are mentioned frequently in Pope's poems. In order to save space, repetitious notes have been avoided. Readers who fail to find a name explained in the notes to one poem are advised to glance at the notes to other poems, especially those earlier in the book. Some political references are explained in Part 1, especially in the sections on historical background and Pope's politics.

The Rape of the Lock

The first version of *The Rape of the Lock* was published in 1712, a year after the incident on which the poem was based. Pope's friend, John Caryll, asked him to write the poem to end the quarrel begun when the young Lord Petre (1690–1713) cut off a lock of Arabella Fermor's hair. All these people belonged to fashionable Roman Catholic families and this may have a bearing on the extensive use of religious ritual in the poem. The work was originally in two parts, but Pope added the sylphs, the card game and the Cave of Spleen in 1713 and Clarissa's speech in 1717. This fuller version is the one referred to here.

    The Rape of the Lock is a mock-heroic poem which uses the style and structure of epic both to make fun of its own trivial subject and to suggest loftier attitudes. It begins with a passage stating what the poem is about and invoking the help of the muse of poetry, thus imitating the openings of many epic poems. Then follows a description of sunrise in which Pope also describes the lazy, rich society of the poem. Our attention is focused on the heroine, Belinda, and then Pope introduces the figures of his epic machinery or supernatural beings, the sylphs, a parody of the gods and goddesses of Greek and Roman epics. But Ariel's speech is both a description of the sylphs and a further comment on Belinda's way of life. His final warning, 'Beware of all, but most beware of man!' (I.114), brings in a note of foreboding. Canto I ends with the ritual of Belinda's dressing, in which she seems to worship her own reflection in the mirror, thus suggesting her vanity.

    In the second canto, Belinda sets off by boat to a social occasion. While this journey is made, Pope tells us, first, of her two famous locks of hair and, second, of the ambition of the Baron to possess them as love-tokens. Like an epic hero, the Baron invokes divine assistance. In another parody of ritual, he sacrifices tokens of his former romances to the god Love, but is granted only half his prayer, that is, one lock, not both. Meanwhile, Belinda sails on, serenely beautiful. Ariel, however, is worried and gives orders to the sylphs to guard her closely, on pain of dire punishments for failure. Once again, Ariel adds to the suspense of the plot by his forebodings.

In Canto III Belinda, now at Hampton Court Palace, plays a game of cards, described in heroic terms as a parody of the battle scenes in epic poems. Pope implies that the energy and emotion which used to be devoted to serious purposes is in Belinda's world wasted in gambling. At the same time, the contest between Belinda and the Baron at cards is part of their flirtation and shows us Belinda's coquetry. After the game comes yet another social ritual, when coffee is served. While this is going on, the Baron borrows a pair of scissors from Clarissa and snips off one of the unsuspecting Belinda's locks. Belinda shrieks in dismay, the Baron triumphs and the poet ironically compares the loss of the hair to the fall of empires.

In the fourth canto Pope tries to give a deeper psychological explanation of Belinda's feelings. He uses an allegorical method, describing how the gnome Umbriel, imitating the descents to the underworld of epic heroes such as Odysseus and Aeneas, descends to the cave of the goddess Spleen and returns with a bag containing violent passions and a small bottle of quieter sorrows. A problem is to know how genuine these emotions are when they are released in Belinda and what the change from the guardian sylphs to the gnome means about her character, since in Canto I, 63–4, gnomes are associated with prudes. The speech of Thalestris raises further doubts, because of its slight idea of honour. The intervention of the ineffectual Sir Plume provides a comic interlude and makes the Baron's reply seem dignified and resolute. Belinda herself then pleads with him, but the seriousness of her words is undermined by the triviality of the cause and the bad omens she recalls.

Thus the way is prepared for Clarissa's speech in Canto V, which attempts to put the quarrel in perspective, much as one supposes Caryll meant Pope to do when he asked him to write the poem. But Clarissa's words have no effect, perhaps because it was she who lent the Baron the 'fatal engine' which cut the lock. Belinda and Thalestris resort to violence and the elegant ladies and gentlemen engage in a rough and tumble fight more like small children than epic heroes, although Pope's sexual innuendoes make us aware of the erotic quality of this physical contact. During the struggle, Belinda throws snuff in the Baron's face, making him collapse, sneezing. She then threatens him with a long hair-pin and demands her lock back. Ironically, the hair has been lost in the confusion and cannot be returned. Pope uses this accident to provide a suitable mock-heroic ending which is also a compliment to the lady. The lock is supposed to be taken up to the stars to become a new constellation, a lasting and universal wonder, which, like the poem, immortalises Belinda.

The poem is remarkable for the way its style matches the delicate beauty of the things it describes; for Pope's witty use of the possibilities of mock heroic; and for the ambivalence of its moral attitudes. All this can be seen in the character of Belinda. In Canto II, for instance, Pope describes Belinda's beauty in lines very beautiful in themselves and he insists on the power of her beauty to affect any judgement of her:

> If to her share some female errors fall,
> Look on her face, and you'll forget 'em all.   (Lines 17–18)

At the same time, the grandeur of the comparison between Belinda and the sun mocks her pretensions, and the scene in Canto I, when she prepares herself for her visit to Hampton Court, in its allusions to epic scenes such as the arming of Achilles in Homer's *Iliad* XIX, forces us to consider the triviality of her existence, as representative of a society in which 'wretches hang that jurymen may dine' (Canto III, 22).

It is not clear which attitude prevails. Belinda is dazzlingly beautiful, but vain and empty-headed. Pope seems to forgive her faults because of her beauty. Perhaps the poet had to have some sympathy with Belinda and her world to be able to write about it with such poise and accuracy. Later poems show much less indulgence to fashionable society.

NOTES AND GLOSSARY:

(Latin motto):	I did not want to harm your hair, Belinda, but I am happy to grant this much to your prayers. (From an epigram by the Roman poet Martial (AD40–104), with Belinda's name substituted for the original Polytimus)

CANTO I

Caryll:	John Caryll (1666?–1736), Pope's friend, who asked him to write the poem
Belinda:	Arabella Fermor
Goddess:	the muse who inspires the poet, according to classical convention (see Canto V,149)
Sol:	(*Latin*) the sun
Birth-night Beau:	a young aristocrat splendidly dressed for the ball in honour of the king's birthday
box:	exclusive seats at the theatre
the Ring:	a fashionable place for coach drives in London's Hyde Park

chair:	a sedan chair, a cheaper means of transport than a coach and horses
ombre:	(pronounced 'omber') a card game (see Canto III)
Salamander:	a kind of lizard, once believed to be able to live in fire
tea:	in Pope's time this word was pronounced to rhyme with 'away'
mankind:	here, the male of the species, as opposed to womankind
spark:	a well-dressed, fashionable young man
garters:	the insignia of the Order of the Garter, a company of knights
'Your Grace':	the correct form of address to a (duke or) duchess
thy protection:	that is, the right to protect you
the main:	the sea
Shock:	a typical name for a lap-dog

Wounds, charms and *ardours:* the conventional language of love-letters or *billets-doux*

glass:	the mirror
the Goddess:	Belinda's reflection in the mirror
patches:	'beauty spots', small patches of cloth worn on the face, a strange contemporary fashion of female adornment
Betty:	a conventional name for a maid-servant

CANTO II

the Thames:	the river which flows through London
Jews, infidels:	Pope leaves it vague whether it is the symbol of Christianity, the cross, or Belinda's beautiful bosom which makes believers of these non-Christians
the Baron:	Robert, seventh Lord Petre (1690–1713)
Phoebus:	Apollo, the classical sun-god; hence another reference to the sun
romances:	long, extravagant works of fiction, much concerned with love
aerial:	pronounced as four syllables, here and in line 76
sylphids:	female sylphs

Fays, Fairies, Genii, Elves and Daemons: all types of small supernatural beings

painted bow:	the rainbow
powder:	face powder, to whiten the complexion
wash:	a cosmetic lotion
Furbelow:	a gather in the material of a dress, much like a flounce

Diana's law:	Diana was the Roman goddess of virgin chastity
stain:	Pope uses this one verb to govern two objects, honour and brocade (the rich material of a dress), of different importance. This suggests a lack of moral discrimination in Belinda's society. The same figure of speech is used in line 109 and elsewhere in the poem (for example, in Canto III, 8)
drops:	diamonds, probably worn dangling from the ears
Ixion:	punished by the Greek god Zeus who tied him to a wheel
chocolate:	hot drinking-chocolate or cocoa, a fashionable luxury at this time

CANTO III

Anna:	Anne (reigned 1702–14), Queen of Great Britain and Ireland, who also claimed the crown of France
ombre:	basically a trick-taking game like whist, with three players and a pack of forty cards, but with many special rules affecting their values. To win, the player bidding ombre must take more tricks than either opponent. Belinda wins the first four and the Baron the next four, so that she needs the last to avoid losing ('codille')
sacred nine:	there were nine muses, divine inspirers of the arts (see *To Fortescue*, 31); here Pope means each player is dealt nine cards
Matadore:	one of the three top trump cards. The Spanish name (*matador*, killer) recalls the origin of ombre
place:	social rank or status
velvet plain:	cloth-covered playing table
'Let Spades . . .:	in this line Belinda blasphemously echoes the Creator in the Bible, who commanded 'Let there be light!' (Genesis 1:3)
Spadillio:	the Ace of Spades, a 'matador'; Belinda plays her highest cards first, sure of success
Manillio:	the two of Spades, another 'matador'
Basto:	the Ace of Clubs, the third 'matador'
plebeian:	that is, not a trump card
Pam:	the Knave of Clubs, top card in another game, loo
Amazon:	the Queen of Spades; the Amazons were a legendary nation of warlike women
Club's black tyrant:	the King of Clubs
Codille:	see 'ombre' above
Ace of Hearts:	inferior to the King of Hearts in this game
berries:	coffee beans, here roasted and ground in a mill

altars of Japan:	lacquered tables
China's earth:	a mock-heroic way of referring to the porcelain cups
Scylla:	daughter of Nisus. According to the Roman poet Ovid (43BC–AD18), she took from her father's head the unique purple hair which guaranteed the safety of his kingdom. As punishment she was turned into a bird
Forfex:	scissors, the 'two-edged weapon' of line 128
wreaths of triumph:	laurel wreaths, awarded to victorious generals by the ancient Greeks and Romans
six:	that is, six horses, usually matched for colour
Atalantis:	a book of scandalous stories, disguised as fiction, published by Mrs Manley (1663–1724) in 1709
receives its date:	is brought to an end
Troy:	the successful siege of Troy by the Greeks is the scene of Homer's epic poem, the *Iliad*

CANTO IV

manteau:	a mantua or loose gown
Cave of Spleen:	Ovid had described the Cave of Envy in his Latin poem *Metamorphoses* and the English poet Edmund Spenser (1552?–99) the Cave of Despair in his *Faerie Queene*, I. 9 (1589–96). Spleen was the name for the bouts of ill-temper, also known as the vapours, indulged in by fashionable people
east:	the east wind was supposed to induce the spleen
Homer's tripod walks:	walking tripods appear in *Iliad*, XVIII
Spleenwort:	a type of fern, used as a herbal remedy for the spleen. In Virgil's *Aeneid*, VI, Aeneas carries a golden bough as a charm in his descent to the underworld
physic:	medicine
airy horns:	horns were symbolic of cuckoldry; here they are airy, that is, insubstantial, because Umbriel slanders marital reputations falsely
Ulysses:	Odysseus, who is given a bag of winds to drive his ship in Homer's *Odyssey*, X
Thalestris:	Queen of the Amazons; here identified with Gertrude Morley, who was married to Sir George Browne, who appears as Sir Plume in line 121
toast:	it was the custom on festive occasions to drink to the honour of admirably beautiful women
exposed through crystal:	Thalestris predicts that the Baron will display Belinda's hair, beneath a piece of glass, as part of a finger ring

Hyde Park:	see note to Canto I.44
Bow:	the bells of St Mary-le-Bow, a church in London's Cheapside, regarded as an unfashionable living area compared with Westminster, where the royal court was
Sir Plume:	Sir George Browne; his speech is fashionable slang, with little meaning, so that line 132 is very ironic
clouded cane:	an elegant walking-stick of many colours
bohea:	a kind of tea
Poll:	conventional name for a pet parrot, a bird usually trained to mimic human speech
Hairs . . . these!:	a startlingly bawdy innuendo, suggesting the superficiality of Belinda's care for her reputation, since the most obvious reference is to her pubic hair

CANTO V

Jove:	Jupiter, the head of the Roman gods; often used as a poetic synonym for the Christian God (compare *Elegy to the Memory of an Unfortunate Lady*, line 11 and note)
the Trojan:	Aeneas, the hero of Virgil's epic, the *Aeneid*, who, to fulfil his destiny as founder of Rome, is forced to leave Dido, Queen of Carthage, although she loves him. After his departure, she commits suicide
Anna:	Dido's sister
Clarissa:	whether this character represents a real person has not been established
side-box:	men sat in the side boxes at the theatre, ladies in the front boxes (see line 17)
charmed the small-pox:	Lord Petre (the Baron) died of smallpox in 1713; Clarissa's speech was added in 1717, said Pope, 'to open more clearly the moral of the poem'
whalebones:	stiffeners in petticoats; see Canto II.120
Pallas:	another name for Athene, the Greek goddess of wisdom, industry and war
Mars:	the Roman war god
Latona:	the Roman name for Leto, the mother of the Greek god of the sun, Apollo
Hermes:	the messenger of the Greek gods, called Mercury by the Romans
Olympus:	a mountain in Greece, regarded in ancient times as the home of the gods
Neptune:	the Roman god of the sea
sate:	an old spelling of sat; archaic language is a feature of epics

a living death: here and in lines 64 and 70 Pope mocks the exaggerated language of love songs; compare lines 145–6. Dapperwit and Sir Fopling are characters in comic plays, the first in *Love in a Wood* (1671) by William Wycherley (1640–1716), and the second in *The Man of Mode* by George Etherege (1634?–91?)

Meander: a winding river in Phrygia

on his foe to die: another innuendo; to die was used to refer covertly to sexual consummation

re-echoes to his nose: that is, he sneezes

bodkin: perhaps a hair-pin; it is given a mock-epic history, like the weapon of a hero

Cupid's flames: the flames of love; Cupid is the son of the goddess of love, Venus

Othello: the hero of Shakespeare's tragedy *Othello*, who is driven madly jealous when he thinks that his wife, Desdemona, has given away her handkerchief as a love-token to another man

Rome's great founder: Romulus, who was taken up to heaven in a thundercloud. This apotheosis was confirmed to Proculus Julius by a dream-vision

Berenice's locks: a Greek myth tells how a constellation was made of the hair of Berenice (pronounced as four syllables)

***beau-monde*:** (*French*) fashionable society

the Mall: an enclosed walk in St James's Park, London

Rosamonda's Lake: a pond in St James's Park

Partridge: John Partridge (1644–1715), a notorious astrologer, made fun of by Pope and Swift. He regularly predicted the deaths of the Pope and the King of France

Galileo's eyes: Galileo Galilei (1564–1642) perfected the telescope

Louis: Louis XIV (reigned 1643–1715), King of France, England's enemy at this time

Rome: specifically, the Church of Rome, led by the Pope and opposed to England's Protestant Christianity

Elegy to the Memory of an Unfortunate Lady

This poem was first published in 1717. It begins with a meeting with the ghost of a young woman who has stabbed herself to death, for reasons which are not very clear but have something to do with love. Because she had high aspirations the poet sees her as too good and pure for this world, hence her early death. He attacks her brother, implying that he has brought about the suicide, although we are left to imagine how; perhaps he tried to force her to marry someone she disliked. In return, Pope curses his family, predicting early deaths among them. He then laments the circumstances of the lady's death, apparently in exile, and, in the poem's most beautiful and consoling passage, imagines the setting of her grave. Then, after a comment on the peace and oblivion of her end, he draws the moral that death awaits us all, even the poet himself.

Two things have troubled readers of this poem. The first is who the lady was and why she killed herself. No one knows, and it seems probable that Pope had no real person in mind. The poem is a literary invention, owing more to the works of Ovid than to genuine mourning on Pope's part. It can therefore be compared with *Eloisa to Abelard* as an attempt by Pope to master a genre, a particular form of literary work; but whereas the story of Abelard and Eloisa is historical and known to readers, the story of the Unfortunate Lady remains a mystery.

The second puzzle is the violence of the passage condemning the lady's guardian. This seems inappropriate in an elegy. But the outburst of strong emotion is an expression of the poet's passion. Similar passionate outbursts are present in the pastoral elegy *Lycidas* (1638) by John Milton (1608–74). Aesthetically, they form climaxes and contrast with the gentler endings. Much of Pope's poem is justifiable in these terms. It is to be admired as a performance, in which the range of emotion displayed and the adroitness of the transitions between different parts are evidence of the poet's mastery. Perhaps for this reason the piece has often seemed theatrical to readers and it might well be compared with an operatic solo or concert aria.

NOTES AND GLOSSARY:

Roman's part: suicide, often regarded, as in Shakespeare's *Antony and Cleopatra*, as a typically Roman way to die

reversion: a legal term, meaning the restoration of property after a fixed period; the sense here is a return to heavenly existence after the interval of mortal life

Powers: heavenly powers, God. In Pope's time, there was some reluctance to name God directly in literature, so that many oblique forms of words were used instead

lamps in sepulchres: see *Eloisa to Abelard*, 261

Eastern kings: Europeans generally regarded the rulers of Asia as inactive and pleasure-loving

purer spirits: a scientific image, from the process of distilling

race: her family, mention of whom forms the link to the next passage, about her brother

the ball: the world; justice is often personified holding a globe

line:	family succession
passengers:	passers-by
blacken:	this combines the effect of dark masses of people with an allusion to the black clothing worn by mourners (see line 55)
the Furies:	the personifications of vengeance in Greek mythology
Loves:	statues of love personified; graves were often decorated with symbolic mourning figures
sacred:	notice the repetition of this word in line 68, with the implication that the lady herself makes the ground where she lies holy

Eloisa to Abelard

First published in 1717, this poem is based on John Hughes's 1713 translation of French versions of the letters of Eloisa and Abelard. The form of the poem, the heroic epistle, however, goes back much further, to the Roman poet Ovid (43BC–AD18). His *Heroides* are imaginary verse letters between famous or legendary people in acute dilemmas; for example, Dido writing to Aeneas after their parting and before her suicide. The form demands a situation of strong opposition between violent feelings. The poem should express vivid emotion with many sharp contrasts. The result is rather theatrical, like a passionate soliloquy, and the element of display may make the reader aware of the poem as a work of art rather than of nature.

Another feature of the form is the poet's assumption, so that he can concentrate on the state of mind of the letter writer, that the reader is familiar with the story concerned. The essential facts about Abelard and Eloisa are conveyed in Pope's own Argument to the poem:

Abelard and Eloisa flourished in the twelfth century: they were two of the most distinguished persons of their age in learning and beauty, but for nothing more famous than for their unfortunate passion. After a long course of calamities, they retired each to a several convent, and consecrated the remainder of their days to religion. It was many years after this separation, that a letter of Abelard's to a friend which contained the history of his misfortune, fell into the hands of Eloisa. This awakening all her tenderness, occasioned those celebrated letters (out of which the following is partly extracted) which give so lively a picture of the struggles of grace and nature, virtue and passion.

The element which makes *Eloisa to Abelard* so successful as a poem and as a heroic epistle is the struggle mentioned in the last line above. This is expressed most fully at the core of the poem, in lines 177 to 206, where

Eloisa is torn between her love for Abelard and her religious duty. The dilemma is sharpened because it involves a conflict between carnal, erotic desire and spiritual, Christian devotion, a conflict central to Christian art and culture. Repeatedly the poem hovers on the border between religious love and sexual love, sometimes, as in lines 205–6, confusing the two, suggesting the confusion of Eloisa's mind.

The poem begins with Eloisa's alarm and excitement over a letter from Abelard. Then follows an oblique account of their love affair – how Eloisa fell in love, why she refused to marry Abelard, how the affair was ended violently and Eloisa forced to become a nun. Next comes a passage describing the convent and its gloomy surroundings, gloomy no doubt as a reflection of Eloisa's own state of mind. In the middle of the poem comes Eloisa's climactic outburst against her own hypocrisy. She then contrasts the true piety of a nun with her own secret imaginings. After a confused passage in which she first asks Abelard to come to her and then commands him to flee away, she turns to thoughts of death and the peace of the grave. The poem ends with her contemplating the sentimental reactions of future lovers to her life story and with a reference to the poet who shall tell it.

The ending initiates a complex process of identification, both of the reader with the 'wand'ring lovers' of line 347 and of the 'future Bard' with Pope himself. When he wrote the poem, Pope was emotionally involved with two women, Martha Blount and Lady Mary Wortley Montagu. The latter was in Constantinople from 1716 to 1718. The emotional tone of the poem probably derives from these relationships, and lines 361–2 seem a direct reference to Pope's separation from Lady Mary (with whom he later violently quarrelled; she appears as Sappho in many of his satires).

Like the *Elegy to the Memory of an Unfortunate Lady*, which it resembles in many ways, *Eloisa to Abelard* is an experiment by Pope in mastering a genre. As such, it is a triumph. Although Pope's artistic control means that he was never in danger of abandoning himself like a romantic poet, the passion of *Eloisa to Abelard* contradicts the narrow view of Pope as coldly classical.

NOTES AND GLOSSARY:

Vestal:	Vestal virgin, a priestess of the Roman goddess of chastity, Vesta; here a poetic way of referring to a Christian nun, similarly devoted to sexual abstinence
Abelard:	Pierre Abelard (1079–1142), a French theologian and teacher of genuine significance. Eloisa, or Héloise, was one of his pupils
it:	a letter

dictates:	(stressed on the first syllable) perhaps Pope puns on the meaning of dictation
horrid:	Pope retains the meaning of the Latin word *horridus*, bristling
learn to weep:	that is, drops of water condense on the cold statues
Indus to the Pole:	from near the Equator to the earth's extremity; the Indus is a river in Pakistan
attemp'ring:	mitigating the severity of
Back ... ran:	Eloisa's great admiration for Abelard's wisdom soon led her to appreciation of his physical attractiveness
the jealous god:	love (see preceding line)
Caesar:	title of Roman emperors; hence, any great ruler
A naked ... lies!:	Eloisa decorously refers to the incident which ended their affair, when her father had Abelard emasculated
The crime ... pain:	since both sinned, both deserve the punishment
the sacred veil:	the symbolic attire of a nun
irradiate, emblaze:	brighten with decoration
Maker:	strictly, God the creator; but Eloisa may suggest a confusion with Abelard, who founded the convent she is describing
my father ... friend:	Eloisa addressed her first letter to Abelard 'to her Lord, her Father, her Husband, her Brother' from 'his Servant, his Child, his Wife, his Sister'
to mix with thine:	that is, in a common grave
the sense:	meaning both the knowledge of her forbidden love and the feelings that go with it
'Obedient ... weep':	from *Of a Religious House* by Richard Crashaw (1612?–49)
Eden:	the garden of Eden in its state of perfection before the fall of man into sin (see the Bible, Genesis)
the Spouse:	Jesus Christ; the otherwise celibrate nun is regarded as the bride of Christ. This mystical use of marriage as an image of religious devotion suggests another side to the confusion of the physical and spiritual which obsesses Eloisa
Hymneals:	wedding hymns
Venus:	Roman goddess of love
Matin:	relating to Matins, the morning prayers in the convent
bead:	Roman Catholics often use a string of beads to help them remember the form of the prayer sequence known as the rosary

Alps:	the great mountain range which divides northern Europe, including France, from Italy; hence, great mountains in general
superstition:	irrational fear
I come . . . flow'rs:	Eloisa's rather conventional vision of heaven's bliss
office:	priestly duty
one kind grave:	'Abelard and Eloisa were interred in the same grave, or monuments adjoining, in the monastery of the Paraclete' (Pope's note). She died in 1164. Their remains have since been moved to Paris
Hosannas:	the Greek word *hosanna* is used as a cry of adoration in the Bible, and hence in hymns and Christian poetry
dreadful sacrifice:	technically, the Eucharist, or sacramental meal of bread and wine which is the central rite of the Christian church, is a sacrifice because it recalls symbolically Christ's sacrifice of himself for mankind in the Crucifixion

Epistles to Several Persons (Moral Essays)

The four *Epistles to Several Persons* were published separately between 1731 and 1735. Pope regarded them as part of a larger project, a series of poems on ethics, of which the philosophical poem *An Essay on Man*, itself composed of four epistles, was to be the first section, the *Epistles to Several Persons* were to be part of the last, and of which little else was written, since Pope lost interest in the project. Indeed, the *Epistles* themselves seem hardly suited to the purpose; as F. W. Bateson says in the Twickenham Edition, 'the *Essay on Man* has cast its distracting shadow over what are essentially four Horatian satires'. When published together in 1735 the poems were arranged in an order dictated by Pope's grand scheme and in the posthumous edition issued by Pope's literary executor Warburton in 1751 they were renamed *Moral Essays*.

Epistle II. To a Lady: Of the Characters of Women

In fact, this was the last of the four poems to be written. It was placed second because the first poem was titled 'Of the Knowledge and Characters of Men'. The rather declamatory passage between lines 207 and 218 refers to the theory of the ruling passion, or the dominant interest which motivates individuals, which the first of the *Moral Essays* explains. Around this passage the poem is divided into, first, a series of character sketches of women, explicitly using the metaphor of portrait painting, and, second, a more serious section in which Pope describes the unrewarding old age of trivial-minded women and then contrasts that with a picture of a woman of sense. She is identified, in gracious compliment, with Martha Blount, his life-long friend and the person to whom the poem is addressed.

The poem has affinities with *The Rape of the Lock*, although its style is sharper and sparer; lines 243 to 248 are notably trenchant and there is a greater awareness of illness, old age and death. Critics have praised the wit of the character sketches, but their relentless accusation of women is unfair and narrow; Pope might at least have hinted that men have similar faults. Nevertheless, the ending has great charm. Who would not be delighted by such immortal praise?

Many of the names in the poem refer to types, not real people. In the following notes only those names which certainly allude to historical persons are glossed.

NOTES AND GLOSSARY:

Arcadia's countess: Margaret Sawyer, Countess of Pembroke, who was indeed painted as a shepherdess by Jan van der Vaart

Leda: seduced by Zeus in the form of a swan

Magdalen: the name given the woman who dried Jesus Christ's feet with her hair; she became a type of the repentant sinner

Cecilia: the patron saint of music

Cynthia: goddess of the moon, which is proverbially changeable

Park: Hyde Park, London (see *The Rape of the Lock*, I.44)

spark: fashionable young man

Locke: John Locke (1632–1704), an English philosopher

Sappho: a Greek poetess of the seventh century BC; here Pope refers to Lady Mary Wortley Montagu, who wrote verse and was notorious for her dirty clothes

mask: a masked ball, at which the guests wore disguise

nice: morally correct; Calista is the guilty heroine of a tragedy, *The Fair Penitent*, by Nicholas Rowe (1674–1718)

Taylor: *Holy Living* and *Holy Dying* (1650–1), popular religious works by Jeremy Taylor (1613–67)

Book of Martyrs: a popular work of Christian history and legend, published in 1563 by John Foxe (1516–87)

citron: brandy flavoured with lemon peel

his Grace: Philip, Duke of Wharton (1698–1731), a disreputable nobleman

Chartres: Francis Charteris (pronounced Charters) (1675–1732), gambler, usurer and debaucher of women

fault:	in Pope's time, pronounced to rhyme with thought
Tall-boy:	a type name for a handsome young lover
Charles:	a type name for a footman
Charlemagne:	king and emperor, who tried to revive the Roman Empire in western Europe. He lived AD742–814
Helluo:	(*Latin*) glutton
hautgout:	(*French*) strongly flavoured food
stoops:	a term in falconry, describing the bird's plunge on its prey
Lucretia, Rosamonda:	two suicides, the first by stabbing, the second by poison
common thought:	common sense
her Grace:	a duchess, it is not known who
ratafie:	peach brandy, much favoured by ladies
draught:	in Pope's time, pronounced to rhyme with thought
Atossa:	Katherine Darnley, Duchess of Buckinghamshire (1682?–1743)
be well:	be on good terms
spirit:	obstinacy
warmth:	hot temper
wants:	lacks
equal:	plain, unmixed
Chameleons ... black?:	who could paint chameleons, animals able to change colour, using only black and white paint?
Chloe:	Henrietta Howard, Countess of Suffolk (1681–1767). This character was added to the poem in 1744. Notice that it interrupts the portrait gallery metaphor on which the poem is largely constructed
Can mark ... chest:	she idly studies the pattern on a piece of furniture
Queen:	Caroline (1683–1737), George II's queen
Queensberry:	Catherine Hyde, Duchess of Queensberry (1700–77), famous for her beauty
Mah'met:	Mahomet, the name of George I's Turkish servant
Parson Hale:	Stephen Hales (1677–1761), a friend of Pope
sway:	authority
Sabbaths:	the annual meetings of witches, said to involve ritual orgies
Night:	visiting night, when guests were formally entertained
cards:	card games, for small stakes, were the accepted recreation of the elderly; see, for example, Chapter 3 of *Emma* (1815) by Jane Austen (1775–1817)
friend:	Martha Blount
temper:	good temper, equanimity

unwounded:	unaffected by jealousy; the sighs are sighs of love from suitors
tickets:	lottery tickets
spleen, vapours:	see *The Rape of the Lock*, IV.16
China:	a pun; both the Chinese empire and a precious ornament (compare *The Rape of the Lock*, III.159)
the sphere:	the world (compare *Elegy to the Memory of an Unfortunate Lady*, 35)
averted half:	compare *The Rape of the Lock*, II.45
tyrant:	a fortune-seeking husband
who wit and gold refines:	Phoebus Apollo, god of poetry and of the sun, whose heat was supposed to engender gold in the earth (see next line and *To Allen, Lord Bathurst*, line 2)
good humour:	see *The Rape of the Lock*, V.30

Epistle III. To Allen, Lord Bathurst: Of the Use of Riches

This was the second of the *Epistles* to be published. The first, *To Burlington*, had caused a scandal because one of its characters had been identified with a nobleman Pope had not meant to attack. In *To Bathurst*, therefore, he uses real names or easily recognised pseudonyms. The poem is thus far more historical than *To a Lady* and shows Pope satirising his own society directly and fearlessly. This tends to make it a series of pictures of the abuse of riches, summed up in the extremes of Old Cotta's miserliness and his heir's prodigality, until we reach the passage dedicated to the Man of Ross, a lonely upholder of moderation and Christian values. In immediate contrast is placed Pope's grim account of the death of the Duke of Buckingham, an effective passage, although quite fictitious; one danger of Pope's decision to use factual evidence in his satire is that he sometimes makes mistakes.

The poem ends with the brisk fable of Sir Balaam, which summarises much of what Pope has said. Sir Balaam, for instance, puts the grossly material, in the form of puddings, in place of spiritual values, just as, in the fantastic passage where he imagines wealth transformed from money into bulky goods (35–64), Pope implies that riches in general are no more than a wasteful mass of superfluous substance.

NOTES AND GLOSSARY:

Bathurst:	Allen Bathurst (1685–1775), one of Pope's more surprising friends, since he was a pleasure-loving man of loose morals. He was, however, a great gardener (see *To Burlington*, line 178)
doctors:	learned men, not necessarily medical doctors

Momus:	the god of fault-finding
its sire, the sun:	see *To a Lady*, line 289 and note
Elect:	the chosen of God. Pope alludes to the Calvinist doctrine of predestination and thus to the connection between strict Protestantism, with its emphasis on the virtue of hard work, and riches
Ward:	John Ward (*d.*1755), a forger
Waters:	Peter Waters or Walter (1664?–1746), money-lender and miser (see also line 125)
saps:	a metaphor from siegecraft, in which trenches or saps were dug forward to reach close enough to a fortress's walls to launch an assault
the Quorum:	Justices of the Peace, country magistrates; hard drinkers all, no doubt
levée:	morning assembly of visitors at an important person's house
Sir Morgan:	a fictitious name, according to Pope himself
Worldly:	Edward Wortley Montagu (1681–1761), Lady Mary's husband
Colepepper:	Sir William Colepepper (1668–1740), ruined by gambling
his Grace:	Wriothesley Russell, Duke of Bedford (1708–32), who lost £3,800 in one gambling spree at White's Club, London
Uxorio:	John Hervey, Earl of Bristol (1665–1751), both uxorious and a sportsman
Adonis:	Lord Hervey; see *To Arbuthnot*, 305
quadrille:	a card game, similar to ombre (see *To Fortescue*, 38)
Patriot:	Sir Christopher Musgrave (1632?–1704); as he was leaving a private meeting with King William III his bag of gold coins broke, revealing that he had been bribed
Cato:	Marcus Porcius Cato (95–46BC), a Roman republican who resisted Julius Caesar's rise to autocratic power; hence any upright opponent of autocracy. Here used ironically
imped:	with feathers inserted; thus a falconer mends a hawk's broken wing
Sibyl:	a Roman fortune teller, who wrote her predictions on leaves which she then scattered
Turner:	Richard Turner (*d.*1733), a miser who denied himself every comfort
Hopkins:	John Hopkins (*d.*1732), known as Vulture Hopkins, who disinherited his own family; see also line 291

Japhet: Japhet Crook (1622–1734), a forger, had his nose and ears cut off in punishment. Such barbarity has ceased to be a feature of British justice

Hippia, Fulvia: probably fictitious ladies

Narses: William, Earl Cadogan (1675–1726)

Harpax: (*Greek*) robber; not identified

Shylock: again, a reference to Edward Wortley Montagu; he was a miser

Bond: Denis Bond (*d*.1747), swindler, involved in embezzling money given for charity

Sir Gilbert: Sir Gilbert Heathcote (1652–1733), a founder of the Bank of England, unjustly thought to be a miser

Blunt: Sir John Blunt (1665–1733), one of the directors of the South Sea Company; see lines 119 and 135

Bishop: Sir Robert Sutton (1672–1746), involved in the charity swindle with Bond

Each does . . . himself: an inversion of Christ's command to love your neighbour as yourself (see the Bible, Matthew 22:39)

Shylock: here, confusingly, Charles Douglas, Earl of Selkirk (1663–1739)

South Sea year: 1720, when shares in the South Sea Company rose in value from £100 to £1,000, then rapidly fell, ruining many speculators, who blamed the directors of the company. The affair became known as the 'South Sea Bubble' (to 'bubble' meant to cheat)

Phryne: a courtesan in ancient Athens; here is meant Maria Skerret (1702?–38), Sir Robert Walpole's mistress and second wife, and thus in a position to know about a proposed tax or excise in time to avoid it

plum: slang for £100,000, as here, or for a man worth that amount

Didius: a Roman so wealthy that in AD193 he was able to buy the title of emperor

Gage: Joseph Gage (1678?–1753?) offered £3,000,000 for the crown of Poland, which was not hereditary but awarded by the Polish nobility. He later married Mary Herbert (1700?–70?), who, before she lost her fortune, had wanted to marry none but a reigning monarch. The King of Spain granted Gage control of the Asturian gold mines

job: deal in stocks and shares

bite: cheat or swindle (see lines 107 and 364)

half-a-crown: a coin worth two shillings and sixpence

Anne's and Edward's arms: in the reigns of Edward III (1327–77) and Queen Anne, England was victorious in wars with France

to buy both sides: that is, please both political parties; Whigs and Tories alike bought South Sea Company shares

Mammon: the spirit of materialism

Old Cotta: Sir John Cutler (1608?–93), a notorious miser (see also line 315)

unbought: that is, he made free meals of weeds

Brahmins: Hindu caste of priests, supposed by Pope to live austerely, like some Christian saints

Chartreux: Pope is using this as the name of any house of the austere Carthusian order of monks, not referring to any specific monastery. The most famous Carthusian monastery is near Grenoble in France

unwilling steeds: the hungry horses of travellers seeking hospitality

Divine: a clergyman, deep-drinking rather than deep-thinking

His oxen . . . cause: the younger Cotta feasts the voters at elections on behalf of the government party

fleet: the navy, whose ships were made of wood (see *To Burlington*, line 188)

our valiant bands: the regiments of the army

train-bands: the London militia, here involved in anti-Roman Catholic riots, burning the Pope in effigy

Oxford: Edward Harley, Earl of Oxford (1689–1741), one of Queen Anne's chief ministers, imprisoned under George I. He was a great collector of books and manuscripts and a friend of Pope and Swift

Man of Ross: John Kyrle (*d.*1724). Pope's account of his philanthropy contains slight exaggerations

Vaga: the river Wye, on which the town of Ross stands. It flows into the estuary of the river Severn

where . . . die: in the Parish Register, where births and deaths were officially recorded

a vile image: a Parian marble statue on the tomb, which portrays the dead man uncharacteristically smiling and offering his hands

Gorgon: one of the three sisters, Greek mythological monsters, whose heads were covered with snakes

George and Garter: badges of nobility

Villiers: George Villiers, Duke of Buckingham (1628–87), courtier and wit; lover of Lady Shrewsbury, whose husband he killed in a duel

Cliveden:	Buckingham's country palace
king:	Charles II (1660–85), known as the Merry Monarch
Brutus:	Julius Caesar's assassin, who, at the point of death, is said to have called virtue nothing but an empty name
But ... 'Agreed':	Pope's amusing transition here suggests that even he did not take the philosophical discussion in *To Bathurst* too seriously, and preferred the vivid examples of the abuse of riches
London's column:	a monument to the Great Fire of London, 1666, which accused the Roman Catholics of starting the blaze
Balaam:	a biblical name. Pope's story is a counterpart to that of Job, who was tempted by misfortune to renounce his faith in God. Balaam here partly resembles Sir Thomas Pitt, a pious merchant with an estate in Cornwall, who bought an Indian diamond for twenty thousand pounds and sold it for a hundred thousand pounds
Change:	the Stock Exchange in London, where shares are bought and sold
farthing:	at this time the smallest British coin, worth one quarter of an old penny
shipwrecks:	shipwrecked goods were a source of wealth to coastal dwellers, who were often accused of causing wrecks to get them
Sir:	Balaam has been knighted; his wife, now styled Lady, insists that his way of life should match his new status
factor:	European overseer (the word 'honest' is ironic)
groat:	four (old) pence
shower:	like the shower of gold into which the Greek god Zeus transformed himself to seduce Danae; here the Devil becomes a tempting shower of share certificates
Director:	perhaps of the South Sea Company (see line 119 and note)
cits:	City of London tradesmen and businessmen, despised by the fashionable, such as Balaam's fair second wife
commission:	an officer's rank in the army
St Stephen:	the House of Commons, one of the Houses of Parliament, met in St Stephen's Chapel
play:	gambling

Coningsby: Thomas, Earl Coningsby (1645?–1729), a Whig who led the impeachment of Oxford (see line 243 and note) in 1715

Epistle IV. To Richard Boyle, Earl of Burlington: Of the Use of Riches

To Burlington was first published in 1731, with the sub-title 'Of Taste', which became, in a third edition, 'Of False Taste'. Only in 1735, when the four epistles were printed together, was the title changed to 'Of the Use of Riches', the same as that of *To Bathurst*, as though to associate the two poems more closely. But although both lay stress on good sense and moderation – 'the golden mean' (*To Bathurst*, 246) – *To Burlington* is dominated by Pope's aesthetic ideas about architecture and gardening.

Thus, after a series of general comments, strongly reminiscent of *An Essay on Criticism* (1711), we come to the heart of the poem, the exuberant satirical description of Timon's villa, a monument of uncomfortable grandeur. The reader is impressed more by its offences against taste than by the abuse of riches it represents and, in the marvellous lines (173–6) in which Pope foretells the return of this splendour to useful farmland, Timon's vanity is surely seen as an affront more to nature than to the laws of economics. The closing emphasis on livestock and tree-planting confirms this. Although Pope's rise to a heroic tone in praising public works in the final paragraph is a remarkable achievement, it lacks the brilliance of his condemnation of Timon's faithless chapel.

Only names which clearly refer to real people are noted below.

NOTES AND GLOSSARY:

Burlington: Richard Boyle (1694–1753), 3rd Earl of Burlington, English architect and patron of the arts who favoured a return to classical styles in architecture and who was widely influential in this sphere

Topham, Pembroke, Hearne, Mead, Sloane: great collectors of works of art and nature in Pope's time; the collection of Sir Hans Sloane (1660–1753) became the foundation of the British Museum, London

Ripley: Thomas Ripley (*d.*1758), architect, whose main fault in Pope's eyes was his association with Sir Robert Walpole

Bubo: George Bubb Doddington (1691–1762)

you show us: Burlington was attempting to promote a rather severe classical style of architecture

Palladian: in the style of Andrea Palladio (1518–80), Italian neo-classical architect

the seven:	the traditional subjects taught in medieval and Renaissance universities in Europe: grammar, logic, rhetoric, arithmetic, music, geometry and astronomy
Jones:	Inigo Jones (1573–1652), English architect
Le Nôtre:	André Le Nôtre (1613–1700), designer of the great gardens at Louis XIV's palace of Versailles, near Paris (see line 71)
genius:	spirit, natural qualities
Stowe:	the house and gardens of Richard Temple, Viscount Cobham (see line 74)
Nero:	Roman emperor AD54–68
seat:	residence, house
Dr Clarke:	Samuel Clarke (1675–1729), English philosopher of not absolutely orthodox religious views, and hence out of place in a hermitage, although Queen Caroline set a bust of him in hers
Dryads:	tree nymphs in Greek mythology
Timon's villa:	probably a combination of the faults of several great houses, including Walpole's at Houghton; but Pope's first readers assumed he meant to attack Cannons, the Duke of Chandos's house. The confusion and embarrassment determined Pope to make specific allusions in his future satires
Brobdignag:	properly Brobdingnag, the land of giants in Swift's *Gulliver's Travels* (1726)
down:	the Downs are chalky, treeless expanses in southern England (see also line 189)
behold the wall!:	Pope's ideal was a garden without obvious boundaries which seemed to merge with the surrounding countryside
Amphitrite:	(the last letter pronounced) wife of Poseidon, the Greek sea god
Nilus:	the river Nile in Egypt, personified as a god pouring water from a jar
Aldus:	Aldo Manuzio (1449–1515), famous Italian printer of fine books
Du Suëil:	Abbé du Suëil, a famous Paris bookbinder
Verrio and Laguerre:	Antonio Verrio (1639–1707) and Louis Laguerre (1663–1721), painters of rich ceilings at Windsor and Blenheim
soft dean:	Knightly Chetwood (1650–1720), James II's chaplain, who refused to name hell in a sermon preached before the royal court

Tritons:	water outlets in the shape of the sea god Triton, son of Poseidon and Amphitrite, and often portrayed as half man, half dolphin
Sancho's dread doctor:	in *Don Quixote* (1605–15), by the Spanish author Miguel de Cervantes (1547–1616), Part II, Chapter 47, a doctor sends away as unhealthy every dish of food brought before the hungry Sancho Panza
God bless the King:	the words of the royal toast which mark the end of the meal; Pope compresses the banquet into one line
Ceres:	Roman goddess of the crops
Boyle:	see title
Vitruvius:	Marcus Pollio Vitruvius, the first century BC Roman author of the only surviving classical book on architecture

Epistle to Dr Arbuthnot: Prologue to the Satires

This poem was published in 1735. It was hurriedly put together (many passages had been composed, and even published, much earlier) because John Arbuthnot (1667–1735), Pope's friend and physician, collaborator in several works, was evidently dying. Yet the poem is one of Pope's best for its memorable lines, satirical portraits and the easy, unaffected tone, in which Pope imitates the Roman poet Horace.

The epistle begins by concentrating on bad poets who write for the wrong reasons. We are led to sympathise with Pope because he is tormented by such fools. We are prepared to agree that to punish them Pope should name them in his satire, which brings us to the central question, one Arbuthnot himself raised with Pope, whether it is wise or safe for the satirist to attack real people. Pope delays his answer, first giving an account of his literary career, in which he emphasises his forbearance and the animosity of his critics, including even the apparently fair-minded Atticus. The effect is to justify Pope's assertion that when he does make an attack he has good reason and a genuine sense of moral outrage. From line 334 for nearly thirty lines he scathingly denounces all sorts of vice, concluding 'a knave's a knave, to me, in every state'.

Immediately, however, he descends from this elevated position, to recount how little he has resented the attacks on him, although offended by aspersions on his family. In reply to these, he presents an account of his father, dignified into an emblem of Horatian moderation, and ends with a sympathetic picture of his own care for his dying mother. The whole poem is a skilful, and successful, bid to win over the reader. It goes beyond autobiography to present an image of Pope as a poet in the admired classical mould of Horace, and it justifies his role as a satirist.

In his 1751 edition, Warburton added the phrase 'Prologue to the Satires' to the title of the poem. This at least has the merit of associating *To Arbuthnot* with Pope's other Horatian poems.

NOTES AND GLOSSARY:

John:	John Serle, Pope's servant
Dog Star:	Sirius, associated with madness (hence Bedlam, the London madhouse; see line 19) and with poetry rehearsals in ancient Rome (hence Parnassus; see line 231)
Sabbath-day:	day of rest
Mint:	a south London locality, where Henry VIII (1509–47) had once had a coin-making mint, and where, because of a legal anomaly, debtors were safe from arrest, as they were on Sundays, too. They could therefore leave the sanctuary of the Mint on that day of the week
Twit'nam:	Twickenham, near London, where Pope lived. The spelling reflects the eighteenth-century pronunciation
Arthur:	Arthur Moore (1666?–1730), whose son, James, became a hack writer. James Moore is mentioned again in lines 98, 373 and 385
Cornus:	a fictitious name; the word is from the Latin for horn, and so means a cuckold
drop or nostrum:	medicines (see *To Augustus*, line 182)
'Keep . . . years':	Horace's advice in his *Ars Poetica*, line 388
Drury Lane:	a London street, not then very prosperous, partly because of the theatre there which attracted whores and hack writers
term:	the publishing season coincided with the court sittings or legal terms
Pitholeon:	a bad poet; the name is taken from Horace, *Satires, I*, 10, line 22
place:	sinecure (see also line 238)
Curll:	Edmund Curll (1675–1747), a publisher of scandal and stolen papers, including some of Pope's letters (see line 113)
house:	that is, playhouse or theatre
Lintot:	Barnaby Bernard Lintot (1675–1736), Pope's publisher
go snacks:	share the profits; Pope pretends to take offence

Midas:	because he said Pan played the flute better than Apollo, the god changed Midas's ears into those of an ass
Dunciad:	the title of Pope's great mock-heroic satire, which attacks bad poets or dunces by name
Codrus:	a fictitious bad playwright
Colley:	Colley Cibber (1671–1757), actor, playwright and Poet Laureate, hero of the revised *Dunciad*
Henley:	John Henley (1692–1756), an eccentric preacher; he did indeed preach a special sermon for butchers, in 1729
Bavius:	a bad poet mentioned by Virgil and Horace; hence any bad poet
Philips:	Ambrose Philips (1675?–1749), writer of pastorals and children's verse; known as Namby-Pamby. He had been secretary to a bishop. He is also referred to in line 179
I am twice as tall:	Pope's friend means that he would be better able to resist physical attacks by the victims of satire
Grub Street:	where hack writers lived; hence the whole class of such writers
Ammon's great son:	Alexander the Great of Macedonia (356–323 BC), conqueror of Persia; Pope modestly avoids a direct reference to his namesake
Maro:	Virgil
numbers:	verse, because the syllables are counted
art and care:	Arbuthnot was Pope's doctor
Granville:	George Granville, Baron Lansdowne (1667–1735); Pope's *Windsor Forest* is dedicated to him
Walsh:	William Walsh (1663–1708), poet, critic and friend of both Dryden and Pope
Garth:	Sir Samuel Garth (1661–1719), author of a mock-heroic poem, *The Dispensary* (1699)
Swift:	Jonathan Swift (1667–1745), Dean of St Patrick's, Dublin (the capital of Ireland); poet, Tory pamphleteer and satirist, and Pope's greatest literary friend and collaborator
Talbot:	Charles Talbot, Duke of Shrewsbury (1660–1718) (see *Epilogue*, II. 79)
Somers:	John, Baron Somers (1651–1716), a leading Whig politician
Sheffield:	John Sheffield, Earl of Musgrave, Duke of Buckingham and Normanby (1648–1721); Pope published an edition of his poems in 1723

Burnet: Thomas Burnet (1694–1753), follower of Addison; he wrote attacks on Pope

Oldmixon: John Oldmixon (1673–1742), who also wrote attacks on Pope and his poems

Cooke: Thomas Cooke (1703–56), another writer against Pope

soft were my numbers: Pope's first published poems were pastorals, not satires

Fanny: Lord Hervey (see line 305)

Gildon: Charles Gildon (1665–1724), a writer who attacked Pope's poems

Dennis: John Dennis (1657–1734), by no means a bad critic, although he quarrelled with Pope

the rod: that is, the metaphorical instrument of chastisement

Bentley: Richard Bentley (1662–1742) edited Milton, cutting out many lines; he was a great classical scholar who failed to approve of Pope's version of Homer's Greek

Tibbald: Lewis Theobald (1688–1744) edited Shakespeare and criticised Pope's edition

Tate: Nahum Tate (1652–1715), Poet Laureate from 1692, but not a great poet. Pope's line is probably ironical

Addison: Joseph Addison (1672–1719), part author of the influential *Spectator*, a magazine which affected taste and literature for a century. Pope wrote a prologue for his play *Cato*, on the life of the Roman republican, but the two quarrelled over the translation of Homer. The character of Atticus (lines 193–214) is based on Addison

the Turk: the Sultan, who was said, on his accession, to execute his brothers to remove potential rivals for his throne

obliged: in Pope's day this was pronounced to rhyme with beseiged

Templars: law students, who studied in a London district called the Temple

claps: the advertising posters of publishers, sometimes printed with red lettering (rubric)

George: George II (1683–1760); see *To Fortescue*, line 34 and *To Augustus*

orange: theatregoers often ate oranges at a play

Bufo: a character containing features of George Bubb Dodington and the Earl of Halifax (1661–1715)

forked hill:	Parnassus, the hill in Greece sacred to Apollo and the Muses. It has two summits and a spring called Castaly (see line 230), whose water inspired the drinker with poetry
Pindar:	Greek lyric poet (522–442BC); but Pope is really ridiculing those who blindly admire broken Greek statues
day's defence:	a short-lived poem of flattery
Gay:	John Gay (1685–1732), poet and friend of Pope, whose patron was the Duke of Queensberry
'To live ... to do':	From *Of Prudence*, by Sir John Denham (1615–69)
Balbus:	Viscount Dupplin, a very talkative man
Sir Will:	Sir William Yonge (*d*.1755) (see *Epilogue*, I.13)
Dean and silver bell ... never there:	(see *To Burlington*, lines 149, 141 and 99 and notes) here Pope refers to the damaging rumour about the Timon's villa passage in that poem
Sporus:	John, Baron Hervey of Ickworth (1696–1743), favourite of Queen Caroline and Walpole. With Lady Mary Wortley Montagu, he attacked Pope in verse and prose. He is the second Curll in line 380, and elsewhere appears as 'Fanny', because he was effeminate (see lines 324 and 329). In Milton's *Paradise Lost*, IV, Satan, transformed into a toad, whispers evil into the sleeping Eve's ear (see also line 330). The reference is to Hervey's intimacy with the Queen
Rabbins:	Jewish theologians
Cherub:	a type of angel
stooped:	a falcon 'stoops' when it falls on its prey: Pope is referring to his change from pastoral verse to satire
The Libel'd ... Shape:	Pope is referring to malicious jokes about his deformity
the last:	death, the last thing in life
Knight of the Post:	one who lived by giving false evidence for money
Knight of the shire:	a member of Parliament for an English county
Welsted:	Leonard Welsted (1688–1747), another who quarrelled with Pope
Budgell:	Eustace Budgell (1688–1737), said to have forged a will in his favour. He accused Pope of contributing to the *Grub-Street Journal*
Bestia:	a Roman consul who was bribed to make peace; perhaps Pope refers to the Duke of Marlborough
innoxious:	innocent and harmless

Schoolman:	a late medieval philosopher or logician
the sky:	heaven
a Queen:	Arbuthnot had been Queen Anne's doctor

The Imitations of Horace

In 1733 Pope published the first of a series of imitations of poems by the Roman poet Quintus Horatius Flaccus (65–8BC). These are not really translations. Although he often keeps close to the original Latin, which was printed beside his English in the early editions, Pope adds and expands and, more significantly, substitutes names and incidents from his own time. Pope could defend these topical references by saying he was using them only to make his version of Horace more lively. But he also implied, of course, that the moral judgements passed by the poems had the authority of a great classical author. To his enemies he could say that his imitations were only literary exercises; but to his friends he could point out how neatly Horace could be made to condemn the vices of the time.

Pope's prime achievement in the *Imitations*, then, is his success in using the original as the starting-point for sharp satire. Pope's ability to find amusing correspondences between his time and Horace's makes his poems lively enough to be read for themselves. His secondary achievement has to do with the tone of the *Imitations*. It is no easy thing to retain the reader's interest in long poems which, like Horace's satires and epistles, have no obvious structure and move from one subject to another with barely perceptible transitions. Pope masters this Horatian art and, although his tone is a little more formal and less mild than the original, he successfully presents himself as engaged in gentlemanly conversation, sometimes joking, sometimes moralising, always pleasant, never far from serious concern with matters of principle.

To Mr Fortescue (Horace, Satires II, 1)

This was the first of the *Imitations of Horace*. Its argument is similar to that of the *Epistle to Arbuthnot*. Pope begins slyly by expressing surprise that his poems (he is thinking particularly of the *Epistles to Several Persons*) have given offence. His friend bluntly tells him to stop writing, or, if he must write, to write poems flattering the King. Pope replies, first, that the King is notoriously uninterested in literature and, second, that he is forced to write by an overwhelming, but impartial, sense of virtue. Pope rises, with Horace, to a ringing declaration that he is 'to virtue only, and her friends, a friend'. The friend's response, that he should be careful because his opponents might use the law against him, seems, despite its legal jargon, by comparison weak and worldly. Pope both wins his approval and thereby shows us his friend's lack of principle by hinting that Sir Robert Walpole, the King's chief minister, would protect him (this is a joke, because Pope and Walpole were politically opposed; but Sir Robert could in fact hardly object to a poem which followed Horace in praising virtue and condemning lawless libels).

The poem is excellent for the way it imitates the original in handling the objections of the poet's well-meaning friend, whose prudent advice emphasises the poet's courage and integrity. It is significant also in terms of Pope's biography, coming just when he needed to make clear to the public why he was moving from the philosophical material of *An Essay on Man* (published in the same year) to writing political satire. The aptness of the imitation to Pope's own situation is part of its wit, as it is of the other imitations.

NOTES AND GLOSSARY:

Counsel:	a barrister, a lawyer specialising in court cases. William Fortescue (1687–1749) was a Whig lawyer and colleague of Walpole to whom Pope often went for legal advice
as you use:	as is your custom
lettuce and cowslip wine:	said, like hartshorn (line 20), to induce sleep
probatum est:	(*Latin*) it is proved; a legal formula
Celsus:	Roman medical writer; here any eminent doctor is meant
the bays:	the laurels, that is, the Poet Laureateship
Brunswick:	George II belonged to the House of Brunswick. Notice how Pope repeats the vowel sound of the first syllable in the surrounding lines, to ridicule the hollow pomp of Sir Richard Blackmore's and Budgell's patriotic verse
Amelia:	a princess, third child of George II and Queen Caroline
twice a year:	the Poet Laureate (from 1730 to 1757 it was Colley Cibber) had to write poems for the New Year and the King's birthday
quadrille:	see *To Bathurst*, line 64. The following lines contain further references, as do lines 103–4
Scarsdale:	Nicholas Leke, Earl of Scarsdale (1682–1736)
Darty:	Charles Dartineuf (1664–1737), an epicure
Ridotta:	a fictitious society lady, from the Italian word for a musical assembly
F—:	Stephen Fox (1704–76), Member of Parliament. His brother Henry (1705–74) was also an MP

Hockley Hole:	a bear garden in London, where, for the amusement of the barbarous, bears and other animals were savaged by dogs
Shippen:	William Shippen (1673–1743), a Jacobite MP, admired for his loyalty to his principles
Montaigne:	Michael Eyquem de Montaigne (1553–92), French essayist noted for clarity of thought and style
Papist:	Roman Catholic
Erasmus:	Desiderius Erasmus (1466–1536), a Dutch scholar who criticised both the Roman Catholic Church and the Protestant reformers of Christianity
Save but our army!:	Pope rather awkwardly turns a passage in Horace into a jibe against the maintenance of a large army in time of peace. This was a traditional grievance of opponents of the government in his time
Fleury:	André Hercule de Fleury (1653–1743), Louis XV of France's chief adviser, who tried to keep his country out of damaging wars
Delia:	Mary Howard, Countess of Delorain (1700–44), said to have tried to poison a rival in love
Page:	Sir Francis Page (1661?–1741), a judge with a reputation for harshness
Pug:	a boxer, who would punch, not sting
Lee:	Nathaniel Lee (1653?–92), a tragic dramatist, who spent some time in Bedlam, the madhouse
testers:	sixpences, small coins
a star:	a badge of noble rank
Boileau:	Nicolas Boileau (1636–1711), French critic and poet during the reign of Louis XIV
unpensioned:	drawing no income from the state and therefore politically independent
grotto:	Pope's gardens included an underground passage, decorated with coloured stones, which actually ran beneath the road to London
the Iberian lines:	the armies of Spain, defeated by the Earl of Peterborough (1658–1735) in 1705; Pope and his friends liked to think of him as a rival to the Duke of Marlborough, the greatest general of the age
to cover heats:	to smother disagreements
Richard:	Richard III, in whose short reign (1483–5) the poet Collingbourne was executed for writing a couplet calling the king a hog
quart ... Eliz:	the Latin names of Acts of Parliament, identified by a number and the name of the reigning monarch

To Mr Bethel (Horace, Satires II, 2)

In the original poem, Horace introduces a rough countryman, Ofellus, who praises the simple life. Horace himself remains somewhat detached from Ofellus's ideas. Pope, in his imitation, published in 1734, changes this scheme. He begins the poem in the same way, setting the scene just before a meal and introducing Bethel's views with a touch of irony as a bit of preaching. Bethel talks coarsely (see lines 30 and 50, for instance) against both rich eating and its miserly opposite, praising instead a middle way which leads to health and leaves something for the poor. Then Pope departs from Horace slightly and speaks the last fifty lines himself, endorsing a modified version of Bethel's opinions. As in the *Epistle to Arbuthnot*, Pope presents an image of himself, living quietly in the country, enjoying the honest virtues of wholesome food and sincere friendship. He has turned the tables on those who might scoff at Bethel because of his lack of refinement at the same time as he modifies Bethel's rough opinions into a picture of contentment without ambition.

At first sight *To Mr Bethel* does not appear a political poem like Pope's other satires. But just as in those more negative attacks the reader must often infer Pope's positive values, so in this largely positive poem we must infer a negative opposite, the corrupt life of the city, where Bethel's plain speaking and plain eating are despised. The city in question is, of course, London, the centre of government, and any retreat from it is a political act, a declaration of opposition to the royal court and the political machine, with its bribes and intrigues. By presenting himself as an independent country gentleman, even if that means being rather like the unrefined Bethel, Pope implicitly rejects London and what it stands for. As the last line says, he is his own master and therefore the servant of neither king nor minister.

NOTES AND GLOSSARY:

Bethel:	Hugh Bethel (died 1748), Pope's friend, noted for his praise of the simple life
butler:	the servant who kept the keys to the wine cellar
doubt:	suspect; an archaic usage, though still to be found in some English dialects, which is almost the opposite of the normal meaning
curious:	excited only by rare delights
Oldfield:	a glutton, but his identity is not clear
Harpy:	rapacious, bird-like monsters in the works of Homer and Virgil
south winds:	warm winds, the heat of which encourages putrefaction

beccaficos:	small birds fattened for food in Italy; Bethel's suggestion that the British robin and martin might be similarly treated is guaranteed to horrify nature-loving English readers
Bedford Head:	'A famous eating-house and tavern' (Pope's note)
Avidien, his wife:	Edward and Mary Wortley Montagu
presented:	given as gifts or presents
their son:	also called Edward; regarded as mad
one bad cork:	a butler should ensure that wine bottles are well corked, otherwise the wine will not keep
Albutius, Naevius:	names from Horace, not identified with anyone
intestine:	a pun; intestine war means civil war, but here the word also means the digestive organs
ween:	believe; an archaic word to make Bethel seem provincial
coxcomb:	cock's comb, used to decorate food; but the word also means a fool or a show-off
Trustees:	perhaps creditors, or the legal guardians of a young man's inheritance
a rope:	to hang yourself with
new-built churches:	several were discovered in Pope's time to have unsure foundations
Whitehall:	a royal palace in London which was destroyed by fire at the end of the seventeenth century and never re-built
M**o:	the Duchess of Marlborough; in fact she reduced to four per cent the interest on her loan to the government
equal:	unprejudiced
South Sea days:	1720, the year of the South Sea Bubble, in which Pope lost money
excised:	taxed
rented land:	in 1718 Pope moved from Binfield, in Windsor Forest, where his father had moved from London in 1700, to Twickenham, where he rented a house and gardens by the river Thames from Thomas Vernon (see line 166)
Hounslow:	not three miles north of Twickenham
Banstead:	about twelve miles south west of Twickenham and famous for its sheep pastures
healths:	that is, toasts; see *The Rape of the Lock*, IV. 109
double-taxed:	Roman Catholics like Pope paid extra taxes
Chancery:	one of the London law courts, notorious for its delays

Bacon:	Sir Francis Bacon (1561–1626), famous for his scientific writings. His family house came to be owned by Lord Grimston, author of a foolish play
Helmsley:	the Duke of Buckingham's house, sold to a London banker, a knight of the city, not the court

---

To Lord Bolingbroke (Horace, Epistles I, 1)

This imitation is addressed to Henry St John, Viscount Bolingbroke (1678–1751), who had been a leading minister under Queen Anne but was ousted with the other Tories when George I and the Hanoverian dynasty came to power. He was driven into exile in France. In 1723 he returned and was pardoned, but denied his seat in Parliament. For twelve years he tried to organise the opposition to Sir Robert Walpole and the Whigs. During this time he lived near Pope and influenced his politics and philosophy (see line 177). In 1735 he admitted defeat and went back to France. He visited England in the year this poem was published, 1738.

The work, therefore, has several themes. First, there is friendship and the affectionate banter of two men who know each other well; this dominates the opening and close. Next, there is philosophy; after the introduction, the first half of the poem discusses the pursuit of wisdom and virtue. But this theme merges into another, the political, with the attack on wealth and corruption. In the second half of the poem, Pope portrays a society almost mad for money, with the king at the centre. In all this, the wonder is that he follows Horace very closely, brilliantly converting Horace's relationship with his patron Maecenas into his own with Bolingbroke. His chief addition is the layer of political allusion, which is very complex and subtle. The examples in lines 95 and 96 give some idea of how the *Imitations* must have been read in Pope's time, when the knowledgeable would have recognised Pope's use of key political words and appreciated his dexterity in sliding them into his verse. For us today, the marvel of the poem is the way it moves imperceptibly from one centre of interest to another, a quality best understood by analogies with music or the composition of an elaborate picture, for instance by Velasquez or Cézanne.

NOTES AND GLOSSARY:

the Sabbath:	the day of rest; here Pope means his old age (he was forty-nine)
Lord Mayor's horse:	Blackmore's plodding verse is likened to the slow horse used by the Lord Mayor of London in processions, not to Pegasus, the winged horse of Greek mythology
doctors:	learned men (see *To Bathurst*, line 1)

Lyttleton:	George Lyttleton (1709–73), a rising young politician and friend of Pope
Aristippus:	a Greek philosopher, mentioned here by Horace, but also Bolingbroke's favourite; he taught the supreme virtue of pleasure
St Paul:	the Christian saint, author of several letters in the New Testament of the Bible; Pope may have in mind his saying 'I am made all things to all men' (1 Corinthians 9:22)
candour:	freedom from prejudice
twenty-one:	the age at which a young man became free of parental authority
that task:	learning to be virtuous
lynx:	a cat-like animal, proverbially sharp-eyed; Pope's sight was impaired by cataract in his last years
Mead, Cheselden:	two eminent doctors who attended Pope
puppy:	irresponsible young man
bear:	a man of little taste or politeness, as the Germans (Pope calls them the Dutch) were thought to be; note that George II was a German
figure:	superior social standing
either India:	the West Indies or the East Indies, both sources of wealth
admires:	longs for in an irrational way
low St James's, high St Paul:	two London churches, the first more austere in its mode of worship
notches sticks:	the financial accounts of the Exchequer were still kept by the medieval method of notching tally sticks rather than by making written records
Barnard:	Sir John Barnard (1685–1764), MP for the City of London and noted for his upright morality
harness:	the Order of the Garter, given to Henry de Grey, Duke of Kent (known as Bug, because he stank)
Dorimant:	a fictitious character; the name is from Etherege's play, *The Man of Mode* (1676)
D*l:	not clearly identified, though certainly a nobleman, unlike the worthy Barnard
screen:	a word used of Sir Robert Walpole, because he resisted demands for a public examination of the South Sea Company directors
wall of brass:	a close translation of a phrase in Horace, but the first word recalls Walpole's name and the last, which is slang for impudence, was frequently applied to him

minister:	the outstanding government minister was Walpole; Pope is clearly calling him an ass. This line is not in Horace.
Cressy and Poitiers:	two fourteenth-century English victories over France
eunuchs:	the castrati or male sopranos of Italian opera (see *To Augustus*, line 154)
S*z:	Augustus Schutz (*d.*1757), a courtier of grave and serious manner
Reynard:	the traditional name of the fox in folk tales; here he refuses to enter the lion's den
farm:	embezzle (see *To Bathurst*, line 100)
poor-box:	container for small donations to the poor, often found in churches
pews:	that is, the rents paid for seats in church
stews:	brothels; the word 'keep' here has two senses: to own and to frequent
bucks:	young men, who here befriend people without children in the hope of becoming their heirs
hundreds:	of pounds, gathering interest in bank vaults, like mushrooms, which grow in the dark, in manure
Sir Job:	not identified (for another use of the name, see *To Bathurst*, line 350)
Greenwich:	near London, by the river Thames
stocking:	at weddings the bride threw her stocking to the guests; the person it hit would, it was believed, be the next to marry. Flavio is probably fictitious
Proteus:	Graeco-Roman sea god who could take on any shape he wished
Merlin:	a magician in the stories about King Arthur
japanner:	shoe polisher
my wig all powder:	it was the fashion for gentlemen to wear wigs, made of hair, whitened by dusting with powder
band:	neck band, an article of clothing
lawn:	fine linen, conventionally worn by bishops; here contrasted with the rough shirt worn as a penance by the devout
to Chanc'ry:	that is, to the courts for legal power over a madman's affairs
Hale:	Richard Hale (1670–1728), doctor at the madhouse
the Tower:	the Tower of London, the traditional prison for traitors and state criminals. St John avoided it only by his flight to France in 1715; his fellow-Tory Oxford was put in the Tower for a time

To Augustus (Horace, Epistles II, 1)

The Emperor Augustus hinted to Horace that he would like to have a verse epistle addressed to him. Horace obliged, but rather cautiously, in a poem which begins and ends with sincere enough praise of his ruler but deals mainly with safe literary topics. Pope, however, saw in this the opportunity for an ironic reversal, because George II (one of whose names was in fact Augustus) was notoriously ignorant and uncaring about literary matters; he is reported to have said 'Who is this Pope that I hear so much about? I cannot discover what is his merit. Why will not my subjects write in prose?' Pope realised that an imitation of Horace's poem would, by assuming an interest in literature which George did not have, make him seem ridiculous. As he says in line 413, 'Praise undeserved is scandal in disguise'. Of course, if George objected to the emptiness of Pope's flattery, he would only confirm that even he could not believe it was true.

To Augustus, published in 1737, is the wittiest and most waspish of Pope's imitations. Where his other poems convert real people into satirical images or heroic emblems, in this work the whole point is the gap between the description presented and what George in fact was like. Pope exploits all sorts of ambiguities and double meanings to remind the reader of this gap. These provide most of the fun in the first thirty lines.

The middle of the poem is about literature. Pope succeeds quite well here in maintaining a parallel between England and ancient Rome. The progress of poetry and the theatre in both have real similarities, especially in the way English literature was influenced by France in the seventeenth century, just as Roman literature was indebted to that of Greece, and in the corruption of the theatre by empty spectacle. Horace's passage on the origins of satire is less happily assimilated by Pope. On the whole, however, Pope succeeds in presenting an Augustan view of English literature, valuable as evidence of his own taste and as a contribution to the history of criticism.

At the same time, Pope manages several barbed comments about the king; for instance, line 206 glances at George's German accent. The praise of earlier monarchs is probably meant to reflect on George's failings. The last section of the poem, with its repeated allusions to verse which flatters kings, is meant as a reminder of the debased political literature of Pope's enemies and, by implication, of his own independence of mind and pen. Pope's elegance and wit, perfectly displayed in this poem, justify his condemnation of the perverters of literature who mean, or pretend to mean, their poems of unqualified praise of George II.

NOTES AND GLOSSARY:

the main:	the Spanish Main, the Caribbean Sea. Spain sought to restrict English trade with her colonies there and Walpole's pacific policies led to many complaints of government inaction in the face of Spanish interference with shipping
arms abroad:	an allusion not to war service (although George was the last English king to lead his troops in battle, at Dettingen, 1743), but to George's visits to his mistress in Hanover
Edward:	Edward III (1327–77), victorious in war with France
Henry:	Henry V (1413–22), who defeated the French at Agincourt, 1415
Alfred:	Alfred the Great (849–901), King of Wessex, who defeated the Danish invaders of England
the Gaul:	the French
Alcides:	(pronounced as three syllables) Hercules, a hero in Greek mythology, who undertook twelve labours or heroic tasks
Chaucer:	Geoffrey Chaucer (1340?–1400), author of *The Canterbury Tales*, some of which are bawdy
Skelton:	John Skelton (1460?–1529), a poet of allegorical and satirical verses
Houses:	university colleges
the Faery Queen:	the unfinished poetical romance by Edmund Spenser (1552?–99)
Christ's Kirk o' the Green:	an anonymous sixteenth-century Scottish poem
the Devil:	a London tavern frequented by Ben Jonson (1572–1637), the poet and dramatist
tumbling . . . hoop:	this refers to the preference for acrobats and stage shows over serious drama in England
compound:	come to an agreement by mutual concessions
Courtesy of England:	a complex legal allusion, meaning the poet will be allowed his classic status even although he is not strictly entitled to it
rule:	Plutarch, the first-century AD Roman historian, tells a story of a contest to pull off a horse's tail. A strong man failed, but a weak one succeeded, by plucking out one hair at a time
Stowe:	John Stow (1525?–1605), chronicler and antiquary
Shakespeare:	William Shakespeare (1564–1616) made enough money as a London playwright to retire to Stratford

Cowley: Abraham Cowley (1618–67), poet, wrote irregular odes, supposedly in the style of the Greek poet Pindar

'Yet surely . . . Cibber's age: these opinions are critical commonplaces, not always very accurate and the sort of unthinking generalisation which Pope thinks is all popular opinion amounts to (see lines 89–90)

Beaumont and Fletcher: Francis Beaumont (1584–1616) and John Fletcher (1579–1625) wrote several plays together

Shadwell: Thomas Shadwell (1642?–92), Dryden's successor as Poet Laureate

Wycherley: William Wycherley (1640–1716), comic playwright

Southern: Thomas Southerne (1659–1746), author of tragedies

Rowe: Nicholas Rowe (1674–1718), tragic dramatist, Poet Laureate 1715

Heywood: John Heywood (1497?–1580?), an early writer of stage pieces in English

It is . . . God: Popular opinion has to be considered, but men of taste judge by a higher standard

Gammer Gurton: *Gammer Gurton's Needle* (1566) an early, and primitive, comic play

Careless Husband: a play by Colley Cibber, published in 1705. Pope may mean that it is as bad as *Gammer Gurton*, and therefore deserves the same popularity

affects the obsolete: Spenser uses archaic words in his *Faerie Queene*

on Roman feet: Sir Philip Sidney (1554–86) experimented with Latin metres in some of his English poems

Milton: John Milton (1608–74), in his epic *Paradise Lost*, presents scenes in heaven which, to Pope and other critics, lack splendour

hook: bracket. Bentley had used these in his edition of Milton to mark passages he thought the blind poet had not authorised

th' affected fool . . . School: George II was fond of boasting how he hated reading, especially as a boy

either Charles: Charles I (reigned 1625–49) and Charles II (reigned 1660–85)

Sprat: Thomas Sprat, Bishop of Rochester (1635–1713), minor poet and prose writer

Carew: (pronounced Carey) Thomas Carew (1598?–1639?), lyric poet

Sedley: Sir Charles Sedley (1639–1701), lyric poet

miscellanies: anthologies of verse and prose, a common way of publishing short literary works

Avon:	the river at Shakespeare's birthplace; Pope is alluding to his edition of the plays, in which he had pointed out lines he thought bad
Betterton:	Thomas Betterton (1635?–1710), tragic actor, friend of Pope
Booth:	Barton Booth (1681–1733), tragic actor (see line 334)
Merlin's prophecy:	John Partridge, the astrologer (see *The Rape of the Lock*, V.137), called himself the successor of Merlin, the Arthurian wizard
Charles:	Charles II; the monarchy was restored in 1660, after the Civil War
'All by . . . lov'd:	from *The Progress of Beauty* (1732) by Lord Lansdowne
Newmarket:	still a leading racecourse
Lely:	Sir Peter Lely (1618–80), a highly successful portrait painter
eunuch:	see *To Bolingbroke*, line 105
Now calls . . . away:	a reference to the Restoration (1660), and the Glorious Revolution (1688) in which William of Orange was made king after the deposition of James II; this is rather a pointed remark in a poem addressed to a king
prerogative:	royal prerogative, that is, the king's divine right to rule, as opposed to the constraints of constitutional law on his power
not ———'s self:	not identified; perhaps Pope meant the blank to tease readers and frustrate annotators. But either Walpole or Cibber would suit the rhythm and compare *Epilogue*, II.238
Ward:	Joshua Ward (1685–1761), a quack doctor, well-known for his patent 'drop', or medical drink
Radcliffe:	John Radcliffe (1653–1714), a renowned physician, endowed two medical travelling scholarships
cashiers:	Robert Knight, cashier of the South Sea Company, fled to France after the bursting of the 'Bubble'
long or short:	syllables
unbelieving:	that is, lacking religious faith, as Queen Caroline was thought to be
Roscommon:	Wentworth Dillon, Earl of Roscommon (1633?–85), author of *An Essay on Translated Verse* (1684)
Addison:	compare this praise of Addison's literary works with the personal attack on him in *Epistle to Arbuthnot*, lines 193–214

Let Ireland . . . sav'd: this praise of Swift annoyed the court, for his writings had inspired Irish resistance to government policies

supplied: made up for the deficiencies in

the idiot and the poor: Swift had resolved to leave money to build a hospital for the insane in Dublin, characteristically commenting that 'no nation wanted it so much'

pathetic strains: a pun; Pope hints at the badness of the translation, by John Hopkins (*d.*1570) and Thomas Sternhold (*d.*1549), of the psalms of the Bible often sung in English churches

Pope and Turk: Pope found amusing a line by Hopkins asking divine protection from both Roman Catholicism and Islam: 'From Pope and Turk defend us, Lord'

Waller: Edmund Waller (1606–87), a poet whose versification was much admired by the Augustans

Racine: Jean Racine (1639–99), French dramatic poet

Corneille: Pierre Corneille (1606–84), French dramatist

Otway: Thomas Otway (1652–85); his tragedy *Venice Preserv'd* (1682) was much admired

indulgence: in fancy, because the comic playwright draws from life, not imagination

Congreve's fools: in his comedy *The Way of the World* (1700) even the foolish characters have witty speeches

Farquhar: George Farquhar (1678–1707) wrote several comedies, including *The Beaux' Stratagem* and *The Recruiting Officer*

Van: Sir John Vanbrugh (1664–1726), dramatist and architect; he designed Blenheim Palace for Marlborough

Astraea: Aphra Behn (1640–89), 'Authoress of several obscene plays' (Pope's note)

Pinky: William Penkethman (*d.*1725), a comic actor, who once ate two chickens in three seconds in a play by Cibber

the pit: the lowest part of a theatre, with the cheapest seats

Black-joke: 'The Coal Black Joke', a popular tune, used in several songs

(For Taste . . . eyes): a reference to the decline of taste from serious plays through operas to pantomime

Edward's armour: real armour was used in a lavish performance of Shakespeare's *Henry VIII* at the time of George II's coronation; but Pope's ridicule is as much for the official spectacle as for the theatrical one

Democritus: Greek philosopher (*b.*460?BC), known as the laughing philosopher because of his derision at human folly

bear or elephant: a reference to animal shows

Orcas: the Orkneys, islands off the north of Scotland

Quin: James Quin (1693–1766), a leading actor

Oldfield: Anne Oldfield (1683–1730), a leading actress

birthday suit: splendid clothes worn for a ball on the king's birthday (see *The Rape of the Lock*, I. 23); the phrase now means 'naked', for so we come into this world

Cato: in Addison's play

Merlin's Cave: Queen Caroline's little library in Richmond Gardens; it was not taken very seriously. It also housed waxworks, including a figure of Merlin

Historian: Dryden and Shadwell were both Poet Laureate and Historiographer Royal (but see *To Fortescue*, lines 33–6)

Boileau and Racine: they were to write a history glorifying Louis XIV's reign

fit to bestow the Laureate: Walpole had made Cibber Poet Laureate for writing a political play

Bernini: Giovanni Lorenzo Bernini (1598–1680), Italian sculptor and architect; his bust of Charles I is now lost

Nassau: William III, who was also Prince of Nassau

Kneller: Sir Godfrey Kneller (1646–1723), painter of portraits, including Pope's

Hero: William III, Protestant victor over the Roman Catholic James II

Martyr: because Charles I was head of the Church of England, his execution in 1649 was (and is) regarded by some as a martyrdom

Quarles: Francis Quarles (1592–1644), minor poet. Pope's reference to him and the following lines remain unexplained

Maeonian: Homer was thought to have lived in Maeonia

your repose: a fine anticlimax and a cut at Walpole's peace policy, which denied the king martial glory; compare the following lines

But Verse ... disdains: this could mean either that George despises poetry or that true poetry cannot be made on such an unworthy subject

zeal of fools in rhyme: another ambiguity, meaning either the enthusiasm of foolish poets or foolish exploits put into verse

'Praise ... disguise': from an anonymous poem published in 1709
Eusden: Laurence Eusden (1688–1730), Poet Laureate from 1718
Philips: Ambrose Philips wrote, not of kings, but an ode to Walpole in 1724
Settle: Elkanah Settle (1648–1724) wrote birthday odes for George I and his eldest son, later George II, in 1717
clothe spice, line trunks: that is, be used as wrapping paper
befringe the rails: cheap pamphlets were displayed for sale pinned on iron railings in Soho Square, London, and in Moorfields, where Bedlam was

Epilogue to the Satires: One Thousand Seven Hundred and Thirty-eight

Despite a faint resemblance between the opening of the first dialogue and that of Horace's third satire of the second book, these poems, published as the title suggests in 1738, are not imitations. Indeed, the ferocity of the satire breaks away from the Horatian style, whose defence is put in the mouth of the timid friend. He it is who argues, in the first dialogue, that Pope should moderate his attacks because he is offending the government. Pope replies that he thinks Sir Robert Walpole can see a joke. The friend agrees, but thinks there are limits; Pope should avoid unnecessary ill-will by attacking people who will in any case never reform. Pope replies that this will weaken his satire, but the friend argues that he can still attack dead men and those who have fallen from power. This allows Pope to close the argument by defining the real purpose of satire not merely as attacking but as showing the effect of bad examples and how the immorality of the rich and powerful corrupts all society.

The first dialogue is very like To Fortescue, except that the friend's advice seems more cowardly, even immoral; Pope's contempt for his lack of principle is stronger and the final assertion of Pope's disgust with society seems more strident. The break with Horace is clearly meant to show that England is in too serious a state for the mild satire of the Horatian kind. The climactic image of vice riding in triumph, like a pagan idol, is apocalyptic or like the denunciation of an Old Testament prophet.

The same fierce spirit fills the second dialogue. The friend's arguments are again weak. Pope disposes of his concern about naming names and his prudent suggestion to limit the scope of the satire. In return Pope claims he is truthful and praises when he can, but there are few enough to praise. Even then, he is blamed for praising those who are out of favour. No wonder, then, if he attacks his attackers. The friend argues that many of Pope's victims have done him no harm, but Pope, after a revolting analogy suggesting the interrelatedness of vicious minds, asserts once more his concern for general morality. The friend accuses him of arrogance. Pope does not deny it, but tries to transcend the charge by proclaiming not his personal but his professional merit, as a poet and satirist, inspired by truth, fighting, single-handed, for virtue. The friend takes fright at Pope's passionate seriousness, and lamely recommends that he go back to writing general philosophical poems, which can offend nobody in particular.

There are two changes in Pope's attitudes in these poems. In the first dialogue he almost has a good word to say for Walpole (see lines 29–32); in the second, he praises Whigs as well as Tories and fails to refute the friend's hint that the difference is whether they are in power or not (lines 122–7). These are signs of disillusionment with the party political struggle. Perhaps that is why the satire is so bitter and the impression left is of Pope isolated and desperate. Yet his poetic mastery is complete, in the handling of the dialogue within the couplet form and in the astounding range of tone, with a corresponding command of transitions, from the conversational through the sarcastic to the mighty diatribes of the climaxes of these two poems.

NOTES AND GLOSSARY:

Friend: not identified with any particular person

'Tories . . . Tory': quoted from *To Fortescue*, line 68

'To laugh . . . Peter': compare *To Fortescue*, line 40

Sir Billy: Sir William Yonge (*d*.1755), a tool of Walpole, notable for loquacity (see line 68)

H–ggins: John Huggins (*d*.1745), jailor of the Fleet prison; his cruelty went unpunished. He had influential friends

the Spaniard: the Spanish captain who was said to have cut off the ear of an English captain called Jenkins. This story caused the War of Jenkins' Ear with Spain in 1739 (compare *To Augustus*, line 2, note)

screen: see *To Bolingbroke*, line 95, note

Patriots: politicians in opposition to the government (see line 161)

what he thinks mankind: Walpole is supposed to have said 'All men have their price' (see line 26)

Scripture: the Bible; the friend allows Pope to make fun of religion

Jekyl: Sir Joseph Jekyl (1663–1738), old-fashioned in politics and dress

Lord Chamberlain: the minister responsible for censoring plays

Osborne:	pseudonym of James Pitt (1679–1763), a government hack writer
Favonio:	not identified; perhaps fictitious
H—vy, F———:	Lord Hervey and Stephen Fox; Pope alleges the first wrote the second's speech to Parliament on the Queen's death. Hervey then made a Latin epitaph of it
Ciceronian:	like the style of the Roman orator Marcus Tullius Cicero (106–43 BC)
Middleton:	Conyers Middleton (1683–1750), author of a life of Cicero dedicated to Hervey
Bland:	Henry Bland (*d*.1746), headmaster of Eton
All Parts . . . blest:	at her death, the Queen neither received the last rites of religion nor forgave Frederick, Prince of Wales, her eldest son
merit:	that is, in the eyes of the government
S———k:	Charles Douglas, Earl of Selkirk (1663–1739), an unpopular supporter of the government
De———re:	John West, Earl De La Warr (1693–1766), another of the same
Nepenthe:	a drug to drive away care and induce love
Question:	a motion before Parliament
Peeress:	Lady Mary Wortley Montagu
Rich:	John Rich (1682?–1761), actor and theatre manager
his Grace:	Archbishop Wake gave George I's will to his son, who suppressed it for reasons of state
Blount:	Charles Blount (1654–93), a deist (one who believes in God but not in revealed or supernatural religion), who killed himself
Passeran:	Alberto Radicati, Count of Passerano (1698–1737), an Italian freethinker (one who rejects the authority of churches in religion), who wrote a book justifying suicide
a printer:	Richard Smith; he and his wife committed suicide in 1732
gin:	in 1736 Parliament tried to reduce the consumption by the lower classes of this alcoholic drink
Foster:	James Foster (1697–1753), a preacher more respected than the leaders of the established Church of England
Quaker:	a member of the religious Society of Friends, a strict Christian sect, outside the orthodox Church
Landaff:	John Harris (1680–1764), Bishop of Llandaff in Wales

Allen:	Ralph Allen (1694–1764), a philanthropist, model for Squire Allworthy in Henry Fielding's novel *Tom Jones* (1749)
scarlet:	like the Great Whore of Babylon in Revelation 17, the book of the Bible describing the Last Judgment
carted:	prostitutes were punished by being pulled through the streets in a cart
Pagod:	an oriental idol. The word had become an opposition nickname for Walpole or the king

DIALOGUE II

Paxton:	Nicholas Paxton (*d.*1744), employed by Walpole to find libels in opposition writings
not yet:	Pope feared a more stringent political censorship in the following year, 1739 (see also line 249)
Guthrie:	chaplain in Newgate prison, who published extorted confessions, often signed only by initials

Who starv'd ... Debt: see Dialogue I, 112

the poisoning dame: see *To Fortescue*, line 81

Wild:	Jonathan Wild, thief and informer, hanged in 1725. Opposition satirists used him to represent Walpole (for example, see Fielding's novel *Jonathan Wild*, 1743)

drench a pickpocket: unsuccessful pickpockets were often thrown into ponds or horse troughs by angry citizens

if he lives:	that is, if the Prince of Wales lives, succeeds to the throne and is thus able to pay his followers. Ironically, the Prince died nine years before George II
Scarborough:	Richard Lumley, Earl of Scarborough(1688?–1740), a respected supporter of the King
Esher:	the country house, with gardens designed by William Kent, of Henry Pelham (1695?–1754), a government minister
Craggs:	James Craggs (1686–1721), a Whig minister and Pope's neighbour
Secker:	Thomas Secker (1693–1768), a moderate and tolerant bishop, later Archbishop of Canterbury
Rundle:	Thomas Rundle (1688?–1743), Bishop of Derry
Benson:	Martin Benson (1689–1752), Bishop of Gloucester
Berkeley:	George Berkeley (1685–1753), Bishop of Cloyne, Anglo-Irish philosopher
Carleton:	Henry Boyle, Baron Carleton (*d.*1725), a Whig minister

Stanhope:	James Stanhope, Earl Stanhope (1673–1721), a general and Whig minister
Pult'ney:	William Pulteney, Earl of Bath (1684–1764), a leading opponent of Walpole
Chesterfield:	Philip Dormer Stanhope, Earl of Chesterfield (1694–1773), an elegant aristocrat and a Whig rival of Walpole
Attic:	Athenian; Pulteney and Chesterfield were notable parliamentary speakers whom Pope compares with the classical orators of Rome and Greece
Argyll:	John Campbell, Duke of Argyle (1678–1743), defender of the Hanoverian cause at the battle of Sheriffmuir, 1715. Pope was trying to woo him into opposition to Walpole
Wyndham:	Sir William Wyndham (1687–1740), a leading Tory politician
yet higher:	a discreet reference to Frederick, Prince of Wales (1707–51), disliked by his father the King and a focus of opposition political hopes (see line 61)
beaver:	a beaver-skin hat; here the plain headgear of a religious dissenter, incongruously glorified by a halo, or saintly radiance
Lord Mayor:	Sir John Barnard (see *To Bolingbroke*, line 85)
the Number:	those who count as population but nothing more
Richelieu:	Cardinal Richelieu (1585–1642), French statesman
Louis scarce could gain:	even the powerful Louis XIV could not command poetical immortality (see line 231)
young Ammon:	Alexander the Great (see *To Arbuthnot*, note to line 117) envied Achilles because Homer's *Iliad* is about him
honest line:	Cato was a republican; Virgil dared to praise him in his *Aeneid*, an imperial poem
Arnall:	William Arnall (1700?–41?), a government propagandist. The next six lines are obvious lies
Cobham:	Sir Richard Temple, Viscount Cobham (1675–1749), was a soldier, eventually becoming a field marshal. He opposed Walpole (see also *To Burlington*, lines 70, 74)
Polwarth:	Hugh Hume, Earl of Marchmont, Lord Polwarth (1708–94), a rising young politician who, though a Whig, opposed Walpole
a Tyrant to his Wife:	far from being severe on his wife, Walpole was notorious for allowing her infidelities, in return for his own

Verres:	a cruel ruler of Sicily in Roman times, impeached by Cicero
Wolsey:	Thomas Wolsey, Cardinal and minister under Henry VIII. His unpopularity as a tax-gatherer made him another opposition surrogate for Walpole
pots:	of ale; that is, the hack writers are rewarded with drink
break my windows:	this was done one day when Bolingbroke and Bathurst were dining at Pope's house; in the eighteenth century, street mobs frequently stoned the windows of gentlemen's houses
the minister:	Walpole
Turenne:	Viscomte de Turenne, Marshal of France (1611–75). There is a complex allusion here to George II's violent outbursts of temper, which is perhaps why the friend interrupts (compare *To Arbuthnot*, line 78)
P–ge:	Judge Page (see *To Fortescue*, line 82)
the bard:	George Bubb Dodington; the next line is from his *Epistle to Walpole*
the gown:	priestly garment; Pope is hinting at two clergymen who flattered the royal family
florid youth:	Stephen Fox (see Dialogue I, 71–2)
Westphaly:	Westphalia, a German province, notable for pig breeding; Pope's readers would see a slight on Hanover, too
Pindus:	a mountain in Thessaly, Greece, associated with the Muses
in:	in office; Pope attacked gin in Dialogue I, 130
reason on his brows:	the traditional horns of the cuckold
the Bar, the Pulpit:	the law and the condemnation of the Church, delivered in pulpit sermons
Hall:	Westminster Hall, a law court; hence, the administration of justice in general
stall:	cathedral seat; but the word 'goad' brings out a pun on the other meaning of stall, a compartment in a cowshed
eye of day:	the sun, or, figuratively, the light of truth
gazette:	government publication
Address:	the formal reply to the King's Speech at the opening of Parliament
Waller:	Edmund Waller (1606–87) wrote poems praising Oliver Cromwell, the ruler of England after Charles I's execution in 1649

Nor Boileau . . . Star:	in his unsuccessful ode on Louis XIV's capture of the town of Namur, Boileau had likened the feather in the king's hat to a star or comet
Anstis:	John Anstis (1669–1744), the chief herald; at noblemen's funerals, copies of their heraldic emblems were thrown into the grave
* and ***:	George and Frederick
Mordington:	George Douglas, Baron Mordington (*d*.1741). He wrote some feeble political pamphlets and his wife ran a gambling house, but it is not clear why Pope disliked him
Stair:	John Dalrymple, Earl of Stair (1673–1747), soldier and diplomat; dismissed as ambassador to France for opposing Walpole's Excise Bill
Hough:	Bishop John Hough (1651–1743) opposed James II
Digby:	William Digby, Baron Digby (1662–1752), supported James II
what you began:	*An Essay on Man* is only part of a projected series of works on ethics and human nature (see the remarks about the *Epistles to Several Persons*)

Part 3

Commentary

The heroic couplet

Virtually all of Pope's poetry is written in a verse form known as the heroic couplet, that is, two rhyming lines of ten syllables each. Technically, each line ought to be an iambic pentameter, that is, five pairs of syllables, each pair called a foot, in which the first syllable is unstressed, the second stressed. *The Rape of the Lock* begins with a fairly regular iambic pentameter couplet:

> What dire offence from am'rous causes springs,
> What mighty contests rise from trivial things . . .

To preserve the rhythm, Pope, as allowed by the rules of versification, elides or cuts out the second syllable of 'amorous' and slurs the second *i* of 'trivial'.

In fact, absolutely regular iambic pentameters are rare in Pope. He varies the rhythm widely. A common change is to begin with a stressed followed by an unstressed syllable in the first foot, that is, a trochee instead of an iamb. *To a Lady* begins with an example:

> Nothing so true as what you once let fall . . .

It is also permitted to have a double rhyme at the end of the line, and thus eleven, not ten, syllables:

> Behold Sir Balaam, now a man of spirit,
> Ascribes his gettings to his parts and merit . . .
> (*To Bathurst*, lines 375–6)

Sometimes Pope's couplets are highly irregular in their rhythms, as in this imitative passage from *To Burlington*:

> Light quirks of music, broken and uneven,
> Make the soul dance upon a Jig to Heaven . . .
> (Lines 143–4)

The phrase 'broken and uneven' seems to begin with a stressed syllable followed by three unstressed ones, while in the next line the words 'soul' and 'dance' are both stressed and again seem followed by three unstressed syllables.

Similar rhythmic special licence is required in reading the following from the second dialogue of the *Epilogue to the Satires*:

Yes, strike that Wild, I'll justify the blow.
Strike? Why the man was hanged ten years ago.

(Lines 55–6)

The first five words of the first line here all seem to require some emphasis, whereas 'justify' becomes a stressed followed by two unstressed syllables, which, with the unstressed 'the', puts three unstressed syllables together. The second line similarly seems to require stresses on both 'strike?' and the exclamatory 'why', and also on the emphatic 'ten', perhaps the most important word in Pope's ironic reply. Of course, it is possible, as with any ten syllables, to force both these lines into the iambic pentameter pattern, but to read them in an alternating unstressed-stressed sing-song clearly ruins the conversational effect which Pope has so carefully arranged.

These special effects apart, the chief means of varying the verse used by Pope is the placing of the pause, or caesura, which usually comes round about the middle of the line. It may come after the second foot or pair of syllables:

A voice there is, that whispers in my ear...

(*To Bolingbroke*, line 11)

Or it may come after the third foot:

These are Imperial works, and worthy kings.

(*To Burlington*, line 204)

Or it may come at the exact mid-point and thus in the middle of the third foot:

Trees cut to Statues, Statues thick as trees...

(*To Burlington*, line 120)

Here an obvious effect of balance or antithesis is gained. Sometimes, for special reasons, the pause follows the first foot:

But I, who think more highly of our kind...

(*To Bathurst*, line 7)

Occasionally, an effect of climax is obtained by delaying the pause until near the end of the line:

To help me through this long disease, my life.

(*To Arbuthnot*, line 132)

In all these cases the pause coincides with a comma in the text, but punctuation marks are not necessary to indicate a caesura. In this line from *To Augustus*, for instance, a pause after 'worth' would add an ironic effect:

Foes to all living worth except your own . . .

(Line 33)

And of course there are plenty of lines without significant pauses, even if they contain several commas:

Given to the Fool, the Mad, the Vain, the Evil,
To Ward, to Waters, Chartres, and the Devil.

(*To Bathurst*, lines 19–20)

But you might make a case for a pause in the second line here; can you see where?

A further variation possible is the triplet, or three instead of two rhyming lines. There are four examples in *To Bolingbroke*. The triplet, however, is not common in Pope, although it is a feature of Dryden's verse. In compliment to him, Pope uses a triplet in *To Augustus*:

Waller was smooth; but Dryden taught to join
The varying verse, the full-resounding line,
The long majestic march, and energy divine.

(Lines 267–9)

The third line here is another variation. It contains twelve syllables, not ten. This line with an extra foot is called an 'alexandrine', because a French poem about Alexander the Great uses this metre. Dryden, again, favoured alexandrines for special effects of grandeur and emphasis, but Pope rarely uses them. In line 113 of *To Augustus* he achieves an effect of length without employing more than ten syllables.

Heroic couplets seem easy to write, but try the experiment and you will find three problems. First, it is difficult to avoid a dull, repetitive iambic rhythm, and either the pause appears in the same place for line after line, or it does not appear at all. Second, the rhyming word often seems to close the line, and even more the couplet itself, with a resounding thump, whose approach the reader begins to dread. The third problem, therefore, is to merge the couplets into paragraphs. Too often both sound and sense seem to halt at the end of the line, so that the poem becomes a stuttering series of short, unconnected statements which sound curt or trivial.

Pope's mastery of the heroic couplet is often attributed to his overcoming the first two of these problems, but his triumph over the third is frequently overlooked and in some ways it is the key. For it is Pope's awareness of how his couplets go together which leads him to vary their rhythms and control the effect of his rhymes. Like a great chess player who can see each move from the aspect of the game as a whole, Pope treats each couplet as part of a greater scheme.

Pope claimed to have learned versification from Dryden's example. Iambic pentameter is nominally the rhythm of blank verse, used extensively by Milton and Shakespeare. In many of the latter's plays there are passages in couplets which are difficult to distinguish from heroic couplets. Christopher Marlowe's *Hero and Leander* (1598) is also in iambic pentameter couplets, and, perhaps more important, has a classical subject. In a sense, Dryden's work established a long-developing trend in English poetry.

He is significant for two reasons. First, his verse is much more strictly regular. It keeps to the ten-syllable limit of iambic pentameter and is much more evenly stressed than earlier verse. His couplets are also much more closed; that is, the sense is contained within the couplet and does not run on for several lines. The greater regularity gives a stateliness and dignity which in turn leads to the second reason why Dryden is of consequence. In his time the couplet became heroic. For first there was the fashion, after the Restoration, of copying French neoclassical literature, in which the balanced couplet was important, and, second, there was the rise of heroic tragedy, of which Dryden was a leading writer. These tragedies deal with very high-flown characters, whose speeches use a passionate rhetoric. The nearest, more modern equivalent is grand opera, by Verdi (1813–1901), for instance. Although he later changed his mind, Dryden initially favoured couplets for heroic tragedy. This is partly why the form is called the heroic couplet. The theatrical origin of the form is worth remembering in considering such poems as *Eloisa to Abelard*.

But in Dryden and Pope's time 'heroic' was also the word applied to the epic poems of Homer and Virgil, among others. Dryden's use of heroic couplets in his translation of the *Aeneid* points to another association of the term. Both connections, with heroic tragedy and with heroic or epic poetry, gave the heroic couplet the reputation of being suitable for the highest kinds of poetry and the most serious forms of literature. Yet Dryden, by also using it in his satires, especially his mock-heroic *Mac Flecknoe*, showed it had other capabilities.

Indeed, the name 'heroic couplet' is misleading because, whatever its origins, the form has shown itself, in the hands of masters like Dryden and Pope, adaptable to other than heroic subjects. This flexibility is its prime virtue, for it enables the poet to vary his tone through a long poem, thus avoiding monotony. It also means that in a poem which is mainly written in one genre, such as pastoral, the poet can smoothly insert a passage of contrasting kind, such as a patriotic digression or even some satirical remarks. Pope's *Windsor Forest* has such a mixed form and *The Rape of the Lock* escapes cloying sweetness by incorporating the satire of the opening of the third canto. Above all, the freedom to vary the tone the couplet possesses is fully exploited in Pope's Horatian satires.

The couplet itself encourages the contrasting of line with line, or half-line with half-line, which gives scope for balancing ideas or opinions. The verse assumes a judicial tone, extremely appropriate for moral satire, and the opportunity for epigrammatic final lines is ideal for moral statement. Good closed couplets almost by definition need to be crisp and clean in expression and this immediately gives an impression of the poet's refinement and control, both of his medium and of his argument. The contrast between Pope's technical control and the murkiness of the passions and vices he so often describes is arguably the most imposing feature of his satirical poems. Thus the form of Pope's poetry in itself is part of his meaning, and his morality.

The influence of classical literature on Pope

Pope's translation of Homer's *Iliad* is nearly nineteen thousand lines long. His share of the translation of the *Odyssey* amounts to over seven thousand lines and he closely revised the rest of the work. In contrast, the poems dealt with in Part 2 of these Notes amount to less than four thousand lines, and nearly a quarter of those are imitations of the Roman poet Horace. These crude statistics give some idea of the scale of Pope's involvement with the literature of ancient Greece and Rome. His translation of Homer's Greek epics was by far the greatest single effort of his literary career, compared to which his original poems seem almost minor works in scale.

Thanks to romantic critics and poets of the early nineteenth century, who set supreme value on original genius in literature, twentieth-century readers of English literature regard translation as a useful but uninspired literary labour, like writing notes on Pope's poems. They assume that the translator's imagination and expression are constrained by the original and that if he attempts to write with fidelity to his own spirit he inevitably distorts the meaning of his translation. Thus only a writer with nothing to say for himself could want to be a translator. It seems unaccountable that Pope should devote his energies to such inferior work.

Pope's attitude was, of course, quite different. He had an immense admiration for Homer, whom he saw as the first great poet in the tradition of European poetry to which Pope hoped to contribute. As the first poet, Homer had set standards by which later poetry was to be judged. Later poets could show their worth by modelling themselves on Homer's example; some of Pope's childhood poems were versions of passages from the *Iliad*. A translation of Homer was thus a way of showing the translating poet was, if not Homer's equal, then at least a worthy successor, able to match the original in verse renderings of traditional themes – the deeds of heroes, the councils of kings and the judgements of fate and the gods.

It was no disgrace to copy from the ancient poets. It was accepted that later poets could only repeat in different ways what their predecessors had said. The truths of religion and morality were regarded as unchanging. The classical authors, coming first, had expressed these truths, and it was the task of later writers not to differ from them but to recast them in forms appropriate to their own times. This task included translating the classics, thus making them available in more modern dress. It was assumed that what Homer had to say was still basically true and relevant to Pope's society. The translator's job was to make this relevance clear by overcoming the barrier of language, and that included rendering ancient customs in modern terms. On one hand, then, Pope's attitude to the classics is similar to the reasonable Christian's attitude to the Bible; the sacred truth of Scripture is more important and lasting than its written form. On the other hand, Pope's translation of Homer is like his later imitations of Horace, an attempt to relate ancient poetry to contemporary circumstances. Both these attitudes assume a continuity of tradition and civilisation between ancient times and Pope's. Thus Pope is opposed to the modern outlook, just appearing in his time and prevalent today, which stresses the progress of society and the revolutions of history.

Pope, then, looked back to the ancient classics as a source of ideas which he regarded as still vitally necessary for civilisation. He assumed that the forms and styles of literature invented by classical authors were, because of their lasting success, the right ways to express the great truths they contained and hence worth close imitation. And he saw it as the duty and dignity of the poet not to rebel against tradition but to cultivate and renew it, so that it could be passed on to future generations.

Bad writers made him angry because he thought they were ignorant of the classics, or incompetent in preserving the conventions of the *genres* of poetry, or innovators who threatened to destroy ancient traditions. But Pope was on the losing side in this quarrel, for these faults are now the virtue of English literature. Modern writers have abandoned classical precedent and feel free to ignore the traditional *genres* and be as innovative as possible.

Pope's poetic theory

Pope, then, was a neoclassical writer; he wanted to see a renewal of classical values in art. *An Essay on Criticism*, 1711, formulates his theory of poetry. It must be based on nature, that is, on what has been and still is regarded as the truth about things:

First follow NATURE, and your Judgement frame
By her just standard, which is still the same . . .   (Line 68-9)

The continuous tradition of following nature, however, means that certain conventions are well established and ought to be observed by new poets. These conventions are the rules of art, based on the practice and pronouncements of ancient writers, notably the Greek philosopher Aristotle and the Latin poet Horace. The rules are distillations of the experience of nature:

Those Rules of old discover'd, not devis'd,
Are Nature still, but Nature methodis'd . . .   (Lines 88-9)

The rules, and the nature they methodise, are best seen in the works of the ancient authors:

Learn hence for Ancient Rules a just esteem;
To copy Nature is to copy them.   (Lines 139-40)

Whether a poet follows nature directly or indirectly by obeying the classical rules, the result will be the same, but true poetry cannot be written in any other way.

A major consequence of the neoclassical view of art is that it distinguishes between content and expression. The first is permanent truth, unchanging and often repeated; the second is the manner of presenting the first, and this may change according to circumstances. The metaphor habitually used is that of dress. Language dresses the meaning, or as Pope says at line 318 of *An Essay on Criticism*, 'Expression is the Dress of Thought'. With this in mind, we can understand a key saying of his earlier in the poem:

True Wit is Nature to Advantage drest,
What oft was thought, but ne'er so well Exprest . . . (Lines 297-8)

By wit here Pope means artistic creativity, but the word also refers to the matching of the form of expression to the meaning, implicit in the dress metaphor. The second line makes clear that what true poetry says is not something new and startling and that the artistry of the poet is to be sought in the way he writes.

This means that style is a central interest in neoclassical art. From the beginning of his career Pope strove for what he called 'correctness'. This meant not only technical perfection, such as he achieved in his couplets, and the observance of the rules of art. It also meant preserving decorum, or the fitness of language and imagery to the subject matter or *genre* of the poem. The mocking, ironic tone of the opening of the *Epistle to Arbuthnot*, with the use of such everyday words as 'dinner-time' (line 14), would be quite out of place in *Eloisa to Abelard*; and the image of the

Westphalian hogs in the second dialogue of the *Epilogue to the Satires*, shocking enough in that context, would be truly disgusting in *The Rape of the Lock*. Pope would expect to be admired for maintaining stylistic unity in his poems by excluding unsuitable words, images and ideas.

It is for this reason that we need to know in what style a poem by Pope is written. Judgement of *The Rape of the Lock* depends on our appreciation of its mock-heroic quality. Is it enough to admire Pope's pretty picture of Belinda's toilet table in the first canto without seeing it as a parody of religious ritual and of such epic scenes as the arming of Achilles in *Iliad*, XIX? Similarly, do not the *Imitations of Horace* call for a knowledge of the Latin originals, which in Pope's time were printed on the page opposite to his English versions? Virtually all Pope's poems owe something stylistically to ancient precedent, which brings us once more to the significance of the influence of classical literature on Pope.

Does this mean that Pope's works cannot be read properly by those without a knowledge of the classics? The question is hard to answer, although it is vital to Pope's modern reputation. Perhaps the answer is that no serious reader of Pope fails to try to learn something about the ancient writings which influenced him, and readers become serious about Pope after being attracted by the wit and splendour of his verse, which have a ready appeal.

In fairness, it must be added that the problem of literary allusiveness is not unique to Pope, nor is it necessarily an effect of the passing of time since he wrote. *Ulysses* by James Joyce (1882–1941), published in 1922, makes constant allusion to Homer's *Odyssey*; *The Waste Land* by T. S. Eliot was published in the same year with explanatory notes already attached. Anthony Powell's (*b*.1905) novel *Hearing Secret Harmonies*, published in 1975 but set in the 1960s, with references to hippy communes and student protests in Britain, already seems dated and in need of historical notes.

Pope and morality

It would be wrong to leave the impression that Pope's debt to the classics was mainly stylistic. He himself would have insisted first on the moral influence of the ancient writers. Homer and Virgil were admired not simply because they had written long poems but because they had illustrated in those poems great moral truths. Furthermore, as their epics dealt with rulers and national leaders, their morality was regarded as supremely necessary to the running of the state. It therefore had political, even ideological, significance. Dryden and Pope, in presenting Virgil and Homer to their countrymen, were making poetic contributions to the constitutional debates of their time. Whether they had any effect is open to question, although the age was very willing to compare itself to ancient times; even Walpole quoted Latin in his speeches, and Parliament was often called the Senate, the name of its Roman equivalent. The classical ideal remained strong throughout the century and throughout Europe, reaching its peak in the France of the Emperor Napoleon.

More significant than the epic poets for Pope, perhaps, was Horace. Again, his imitation of Horace is not just stylistic but also moral. From an early age he identified with Horace's point of view. The *Ode on Solitude*, though much revised later, is an early poem. In it Pope draws a picture of a life of retirement. He praises the unambitious man, content to live in the country away from the centres of political power, existing simply on what he can obtain in his own neighbourhood, not on luxuries brought from distant places. Such a way of life would bring health and peace of mind, and in the end a quiet, untroubled death.

This idyllic picture, seen again towards the end of the *Epistle to Arbuthnot* and throughout *To Bethel*, is strongly influenced by Horace's poetry about escaping from Rome to the peace of the country, and like Horace's poems it has more moral implications than may appear. Pope is not just praising a life of moderation and self-control, sympathetic to traditional values and avoiding extremes of behavior, positive qualities also praised in his other poems, even those on artistic matters, like *To Burlington*. Like Horace's, his moral opinions are essentially antagonistic. They imply opposition to the contrary values of city life. Just as Horace's withdrawal to his Sabine farm implies dislike of Rome and all it stands for, so Pope's praise of simple living and of his own modest existence at Twickenham implies condemnation of London life, political ambition and ostentatious wealth.

Pope was not the first English poet to use Horace's example in this way; Abraham Cowley (1618–67) and Andrew Marvell (1621–78) had both done so and something similar can be found in Ben Jonson (1572–1637), for example in *To Penshurst* and in *To Sir Robert Wroth*. But Pope's identification with Horace is more thorough and more personal. His own position, acquainted with great men, but barred by his religion, politics and health from full participation in society, made him deeply sympathetic with Horace, the son of a freed slave, who lost his lands during a civil war yet became the friend of the Emperor Augustus.

But if Pope sometimes saw himself as a second Horace, he must surely have recognised occasionally that this was a pose. He may have genuinely meant his poems of retired life, but he was also passionately interested in politics and he engaged in fierce literary quarrels. He was always more active in debate than the detached Horatian attitude would allow. The result is a paradox, which can be seen in another light in his career as a satirist.

Pope and satire

All satirists face the problem that their subject matter, human vice, is at
odds with the purpose of their work, the cause of virtue. Satirists are
vulnerable to the accusation that they have an abnormal interest in
immorality and corruption. They may even be accused of spreading
knowledge of these while pretending to ridicule them. Their description
of the unpleasant side of human nature may be so successful that the
reader is disgusted. The satirist's praise of virtue may be lost on a reader
overwhelmed by the parade of vice. Some readers may even refuse to
believe that human nature is as bad as the satirist claims and prefer to
consider him mentally ill.

As a satirist, Pope runs these risks. His praise of moderation, self-
control and traditional values may be overlooked because it is
surrounded by illustrations of the opposite. Paradoxically, Pope can
appear to be the poet of extremism, self-indulgence and empty fashion
because his works are full of examples of such behaviour. His vicious
characters, like Sporus or Sir Balaam or Timon, are more memorable
than his virtuous ones. And his damning lists of forgers, cheats and
corrupt politicians begin to seem exaggerated and one-sided. Surely, we
begin to wonder, life in eighteenth-century England cannot have been as
bad as Pope makes out. And then we begin to question Pope's right to
set himself up as a judge.

For the satirist always sets himself up as a judge. He claims the right to
pass a public verdict on what he dislikes. He usually, like Pope, claims to
do so in the name of accepted standards of morality. The satirist
appeals, often implicitly, to what is regarded as normal behaviour and
contrasts with that the behaviour of vicious men. But normal people do
not usually dare to insult bad men, especially powerful bad men, in
public; that is to say, they do not write satires. The satirist is
paradoxically abnormal in trying to assert normal values. He is always
faced with the problem of justifying his abnormal behaviour.

In one sense Pope was and is successful in winning readers over to his
point of view. One aspect of the satirist's problem of justification is
stylistic; if he can persuade the reader by his style that he is a noble,
upright fellow, then the reader will be ready to agree with his moral
judgements. Dryden had realised this and in his great satires, *Absalom
and Achitophel* and *Mac Flecknoe*, he persuades as much by style as by
argument. Pope's correctness of style has a similar virtue. Where we
admire artistic qualities, such as wit or technical perfection, we are the
more likely to extend agreement with the artist's meaning. The mock-
heroic style has advantages here, for the poet is not mocking the heroic
so much as using the heroic style to mock the miserable or inadequate
subject. Thus the poet shows himself able to command the heroic style,

able to write nobly and elegantly, if only the subject matter would let him. The reader is given an impression of the poet as a man of taste and culture, who keeps himself apart from the unfortunate human lapses he is forced, by his love of the truth, to put into his verse. Much the same impression is given by the *Imitation of Horace*, where, as long as Pope respects the original, he benefits by a reputation for classical culture and values.

In these cases, then, the style becomes the man; we assume the user of the style has its fine character. Thus stylistically Pope often wins our approval for his satirical judgements. But if we approach from the opposite side of the question, beginning, not with the style, but with the man, a different conclusion emerges. Pope was surely not justified in assuming public agreement with his views. Both his religion and his politics made him an outsider to society, which puts in question his right to speak out on morality and state affairs. His physical disabilities, whether they warped his mind or not, certainly made him different from other people and unable to participate in some more vigorous pastimes. Thus, while it might be an exaggeration to say that a witty, talented, deformed, sickly, Tory, Papist poet would be the least representative figure of the reign of George II, it is difficult to dismiss this view entirely.

Pope's unrepresentative nature can be seen by comparing his judgements with those of history. Whatever his faults, Walpole was a successful minister, with some good qualities, as Pope seems grudgingly to have admitted. George II, though not a great king, was an upright and astute ruler. Viscount Bolingbroke, on the other hand, Pope's 'guide, philosopher and friend', seems to have been a charming conversationalist, but also a traitor and a coward. England, far from declining in Pope's lifetime, was entering on the period of her greatest power and progress, thanks largely to the efforts of the businessmen and innovators whom Pope snobbishly despised. Even in literature there were signs of vitality, with the rise of a new form, the novel, which in time would become dominant in creative writing.

This section ends, therefore, by saying that the debate about Pope's worth seems still wide open. There is a complacent assumption that, having defined him as an Augustan poet writing in the Age of Reason, the nature and worth of his achievement have been described. In fact, he was far less at home in his age than this supposes or the images of himself, presented in his works, seek to show. He is no serene rationalist, working controlled patterns in verse, but a combative poet, struggling with forces which could not be withstood, and struggling also, one suspects, with himself. The question is whether the turbulent passions which contradict the smooth surface of his art and which break out in the *Epilogue to the Satires* make his life's work a pathetic failure or a heroic one.

Part 4

Hints for study

Reading Pope

At first sight, Pope's poems are a daunting prospect – pages of closely-printed lines, spattered with obscure names and broken only by uninformative titles like *Epistle to a Lady* or *Prologue to the Satires*. Pope looks like a boring poet and many readers never go beyond judging by appearances. Yet Pope's works are full of wit and charm and deserve attention for their brilliant use of language alone. The secret of reading them is to read as Pope wrote, paragraph by paragraph.

Pope's long poems were put together from scattered writings produced over a long period. He would write a character sketch, or jot down a pair of fine couplets, long before he found a context in which to place them. The closed nature of the couplet tempts readers to think that each was independently created, and they often read each separately in an unpleasant, jerky manner. It is truer to say that the *paragraph* was Pope's structural unit and of this he is a master. Read each paragraph through first, trying to grasp what it says as a whole. Often the first lines state what the paragraph is about and the last bring to a conclusion the general argument, either in a memorable statement or in a telling example or illustration. Having got the general point, go back over the middle part to see how it fits, for instance, why the examples used are relevant, how they build to a climax, or contrast the extremes Pope is discussing, and so on. At this point begin referring to the notes and glossaries for explanations of the detail. Rarely is Pope's language so different from modern English that it requires interpretation. The puzzles in Pope are his allusions to contemporaries, but these usually fit into a context which is plain enough to the careful reader.

Once you have mastered a paragraph, relate it to those before and after. Many of Pope's paragraphs are set-pieces of description or moral statement, many more are part of groups of paragraphs, such as the series of character sketches in *To a Lady* or the account of a visit to Timon's villa in *To Burlington*. Once you have understood the place and function of the blocks of lines which form a poem by Pope, you will find its general meaning becomes clear and the reading of the poem is enhanced by awareness of Pope's skill in constructing long poems using a verse form, the couplet, which seems so brief and fragmentary.

Take, for example, the paragraph beginning at line 35 in *To Bathurst*.

Pope has just mentioned bribery at the end of the previous paragraph. He now expresses a wish for 'bulky bribes', too big to be hidden. A quick glance through the following lines explains his meaning: bribes in the form of goods, not money. The paragraph comes to a climax with a ludicrous scene in which a politician's servant tells him of the delivery of embarrassing quantities of olive oil, cloth and beef cattle. Now we can go back and solve some puzzles, such as what 'Quorum' in line 42 means. Having done that, we proceed to the next paragraph, which turns out to be a development of the same idea, the fantastic substitution of goods for money. The next paragraph returns to the theme of bribery, with a story of how even gold can be unwieldy to carry secretly, followed by more general moral reflections, building up to a line which ends the sequence, rather as a cadence ends a passage of music:

> And silent sells a King, or buys a Queen.

> (Line 78)

The heavy pause or caesura at the coma here is typical of the closing lines of Pope's paragraphs (compare lines 100 and 402). Such rhythmic effects are one of his chief ways of moulding a paragraph. Look, for example, at the paragraph beginning at line 63 in *To Fortescue:*

> My Head and Heart thus flowing through my quill
> Verse-man or Prose-man, term me which you will,
> Papist or Protestant, or both between,
> Like good Erasmus in an honest mean,
> In moderation placing all my Glory,
> While Tories call me Whig, and Whigs a Tory.

Four of these six lines present antitheses and the last line repeats a contrast in reverse. The exceptions are lines praising 'an honest mean' and moderation, that is, a balance between extremes. The rhythm and the word-patterns thus reflect the meaning. The paragraph is constructed out of contrasts (head and heart, verse and prose, Papist and Protestant) leading up to a final double contrast, which is no contrast at all, Tory-Whig and Whig-Tory, because they cancel each other out. This effect is surely evident to any reader before he asks who Erasmus was, or what Whigs and Tories were.

Answering questions about Pope

Questions about Pope usually fall into one of four classes. Sometimes a question is asked which combines two approaches; for example, 'Discuss whether the mock-heroic style of *The Rape of the Lock* is a sign of Pope's moral confusion about Belinda', or 'Do you think powerful poetry can be found in Pope's cool couplets?' In addition, there are also questions which ask you to relate Pope to his literary period, as an Augustan poet, enlightened rationalist and so on. But the major areas of critical discussion about Pope are delineated in the four types of question outlined below.

Questions about technique and versification, with examples

(1) Discuss Pope's use of the couplet in the *Epistles to Several Persons.*
(2) Discuss Pope's use of dialogue in the *Epilogue to the Satires.*

These questions cannot really be convincingly answered without a sound, detailed knowledge of the poems concerned. In examinations, this means you need to have memorised useful examples. Writing an essay answer, with the text before you, is probably easier. What you must do is collect a set of examples of the particular technique asked for, quote them briefly and say why you find each significant. In a way, these are easy questions to answer if you have a good memory or like compiling lists. But there is a hidden difficulty because in presenting your material you need to organise it and shape it into something more than a catalogue. Stringing together a loose set of little paragraphs, each devoted to a few isolated lines of verse, will make a dull answer. It is much better to try to group similar examples together or point out contrasts and striking changes. In discussing Pope's versification, of course, some knowledge of technical terms is useful (see Part 3), but it is more important to show a sensitivity to Pope's subtle rhythms and to give a clear expression of the connection between what you have to say and the quotations you use.

Even if this kind of question does not appeal to you, it is worth considering Pope's technique closely. Some very good points can be made in answering other types of question by the detailed analysis called for here.

Specimen question and answer

Discuss the use of imagery in *Elegy to the Memory of an Unfortunate Lady*

The most striking images in this poem are closely related to the central theme of the lady's change from earth to heaven. In the ninth line the change is expressed in a legal metaphor of an inheritance or 'bright reversion', but the adjective and the sense of returning in 'reversion' anticipate the theme of escape which becomes prominent as the poem develops.

This theme appears in lines 17 and following, where the soul is likened to a prisoner in the body and later to inactive oriental despots, 'confined to their own palace'. The word 'sleep' in this line also suggests, however, that the soul could awaken, or, to return to the metaphor of line 18, it could break out of the body's prison, presumably to the freedom of heavenly existence. There it would not be so useless as a lamp left burning in a sepulchre or tomb (line 20). This last image is most complex, for it reverses the associations of life and death; the soul in the body is here like a light in a grave and the lady's death is paradoxically like an escape from a state of stagnation or life in death.

A similar reversal is apparent if we compare the image of fading flowers in line 32 with the climax of the poem, the vision of the lady's grave grown over with flowers, life sprung from death (lines 63–6). By its images, then, the poem tries to convince us that the lady has undergone a change to a better state than mortal life. Her memory may be unfortunate, but she herself is not.

Questions about style, with examples

(1) Discuss the mock-heroic style of *The Rape of the Lock*.
(2) What features of the *Epistle to Arbuthnot* make it an Horatian poem?
(3) Pope calls Horace's style 'sly, polite, insinuating'. Is this true of his *Imitations*?

The first requirement here is a thorough knowledge of the features of the style you are asked to discuss. In Pope's case this often means knowing about the classical writers he took as models; Homer, Virgil, Ovid and Horace. You then have to match this knowledge with Pope's poems. You need to know where in *The Rape of the Lock* he is imitating the classical epic, what in *Eloisa to Abelard* is like Ovid's heroic epistles and how Pope's satires resemble the urbane, chatty poems of Horace. The tone and diction of Pope's poems are significant here; what sort of words does he use, how formal or informal is he, and how ready is he to make jokes or use highly poetic language? These things vary from poem to poem, depending on what Pope regarded as appropriate for particular kinds of poetry.

The discussion of the suitability of the style to the subject of a poem is an important development of questions about style alone. You may well be asked to relate Pope's use of a certain style to what the poem says, especially its moral. Questions about style therefore often encroach on the third kind of question about Pope (see below).

Specimen question and answer

Discuss the style of *Eloisa to Abelard*

One feature of the style of *Eloisa to Abelard* is contrast, often harsh and violent, imitating the opposing forces in Eloisa's mind. The most striking contrast is at the centre of the poem, between 'the blameless Vestal's lot' (line 207), described in calm, evenly paced lines, and Eloisa's nightmare state, where instead of melting 'in visions of eternal day' (line 222) she wakes 'to all the griefs I left behind' (line 248). Eloisa's state is described in rushing lines, full of exclamations and disjointed phrases. They are dominated by the first person singular (in lines 235–9 it is used seven times, for instance), suggesting Eloisa's self torment.

The passage includes a scene of Gothic horror, an unpleasant landscape of mouldering, ivy-covered buildings and overhanging rocks. Such landscapes are another feature of the poem. The 'rugged rocks' and 'grots and caverns shagged with horrid thorn' of lines 19 and 20 and the 'twilight groves' and 'intermingled graves' of lines 163 and 164 become images of Eloisa's melancholy, which 'breathes a browner horror on the woods' (line 170). The darkness and dreariness are both an expression of Eloisa's emotion and also, because of their rather theatrical extravagance, a signal that she is mentally unbalanced, and ripe for the suicidal impulses of the end of the poem. There Eloisa's vision of heaven's 'roseate bowers' (line 317) has a similar feverish quality, projecting her desire for the unreal peace of death.

Throughout the poem Pope strives for strongly emotional effects. Eloisa bursts out with exclamation like 'Ah wretch!' (line 177) and 'O death all-eloquent!' (line 335). She uses imperative verbs a great deal, which gives a frantic pleading tone to her words, as well as compressing the language to basic statements – 'write' (line 41), 'give' (line 124), 'come' (line 257) – as though she has no time to be more polite or subtle. This haste is also seen in such sentences as the following, where words are piled up without conjunctions to separate them:

How often hope, despair, resent, regret,
Conceal, disdain, – do all things but forget.

(Lines 199–200)

It is also unclear whether some of these words are nouns or verbs. As in other places, Eloisa's feelings are expressed although her meaning is not always clear, because her emotion prevents her speaking with correct syntax. Thus Pope succeeds in writing a dramatic monologue, where the style is used to convey the character of the speaker and the feelings of the moment.

Questions about Pope's moral attitudes and judgements, with examples

(1) What is Pope's idea of good taste according to his *Epistle to Burlington*?

(2) What comments does *The Rape of the Lock* make on the society of Queen Anne's reign?

(3) How convincing do you find Pope's justification of satire in *To Fortescue* and the *Epilogue to the Satires*?

These are questions about Pope's own ideas. Even where they are related to particular poems, it helps to answer them if you have studied more of Pope's work and are able to sum up his outlook, in matters both of taste and morality. It is not enough to have read the work in question; you must have digested its meaning and related it to what you know of Pope's other opinions. His condemnation of bad taste in *To Burlington*, for instance, is related to his attack on wealth in *To Bathurst*; in both cases Pope ridicules excess and waste, praising what is natural and decent. Similar opinions are to be found in his political satires, where he praises loyalty, honesty and true patriotism, which he contrasts with selfish greed, corruption and party politics. As the third example above indicates, these questions often demand a personal response. You must evaluate Pope's arguments and express an opinion on his judgements. This means your answer must itself argue for a point of view. To be fair to Pope, you must produce evidence of his opinions. Fortunately, Pope is a master of the epigram. All his works contain memorable lines and couplets put in to summarise his views and ideal for quotation in essays and exams. Mark some of these passages in your copy of Pope so that you can find them easily. But beware of complacency; Pope is fond of words like 'nature', 'sense' and 'wit', whose meanings are not often as clear as one might hope. The reason this kind of question continues to be asked is that it is still possible to find doubts and paradoxes in what seems at first sight obvious.

Specimen question and answer

What connection does Pope imply in *To Augustus* between the king and the state of literature during his reign?

In the first paragraph of *To Augustus* Pope sets the ironic tone by praising George II for successes he has not achieved. Among these is the improvement of 'Morals, Arts, and Laws' (line 4). Much of the poem is concerned with the poor state of the arts, especially literature, under George. We hear first how the public is 'partial' (line 32) to what Pope considers barbarous and old-fashioned, and later how the theatre has been taken over by empty spectacle or by 'the Farce, the Bear, or the Black-joke' (line 309). In addition, whereas in the past men lived plainly, now they crowd to the theatres and 'all rhyme, and scrawl, and scribble' (line 188), trying to be poets.

One cause of all this seems to be popular opinion. In the theatre the 'many-headed Monster of the Pit' (line 305) enforces a low standard and popular opinion holds as sacred a number of prejudices about poets, being unable, for instance, to conceive that Shakespeare has faults.

But the reason public opinion is able to dictate literary taste is that writers depend on the public for payment, so that poets aim only to please for money. The poet's need to make his living by catering for low public taste suggests a lack of enlightened patronage, such as the king might supply. He, like the Emperor Augustus, ought to encourage the best poets to write great literature.

Not that there are not many writers who 'expect a Place, or Pension from the Crown' (line 371), but they do so after straining to write poems of flattery. Such patronage as there is, Pope implies, goes to writers of poems praising 'some monster of a King' (line 210), just what *To Augustus* ironically refuses to do. George's lack of merit is connected to the poor state of literature in two ways. First, it includes a lack of the literary discernment needed to identify and encourage good writers. Second, because he is not deserving of praise, the poems that are written for him are pure flattery, shamelessly intended to gain money from him rather than lasting literary fame.

Questions concerning Pope's literary excellence and reputation, with examples

---

(1) What qualities of Pope's works make them poetry rather than verse chronicles of his society?

(2) Is Pope's claim to be a moral judge of his society justifiable or is he himself too prejudiced and arrogant?

(3) Do you agree that Pope's works are too much concerned with his own age to appeal to the modern reader?

In the nineteenth century Pope's reputation as a poet fell greatly. Eighteenth-century poetry in general was disliked for its formal technique and moral doctrine. Matthew Arnold (1822–88), for instance, said 'Dryden and Pope are not classics of our poetry, they are classics of our prose', and biographers stressed Pope's deformities and his belligerence. The twentieth century has seen a more balanced assessment of Pope as a skilful, witty and sometimes beautiful writer, not to be judged by romantic notions of poetry as an overflow of feeling, expressing the poet's own soul. This approach allows us to see the justice of his moral judgements rather than explain them away as neurotic outbursts caused by his bad health. Nevertheless. there is room for deep differences of opinion here and you may well be asked to consider Pope's status as a poet, or the acceptibility of his moral attitudes. Both these points come together in the larger question of whether satire – the art of insult and attack – can be poetry at all. What is at stake is the definition of poetry itself and whether it includes a work like the *Epilogue to the Satires*. In answering, one might consider Pope's use of

language, his imagery, his mastery of style and his underlying moral
seriousness. He can even be defended as a poet of personal expression,
although the feelings he may be said to express, such as anger, moral
indignation, contempt and pride, are not the usual poetic emotions. As
for his moral point of view, the doubt to be resolved is whether his
positive values are genuine grounds for the excess of negative
judgements his satires contain. To put it another way, is the purpose of
his satires anything more laudable than personal spite? Pope himself
tries to answer this question in the *Epistle to Arbuthnot, To Fortescue* and
the *Epilogue to the Satires.*

The third question above is an example of a related problem about
Pope's work. Pope, like all great satirists, was concerned with real
abuses of his time. This may make him unintelligible to later readers.
The conventions of Augustan verse, especially its assumption of a
classical education, also seem to get in the way of modern readers. Of
course, even modern literature may be obscure and difficult; and Pope is
clearly easier to read than, say, Chaucer, or even parts of Shakespeare.
Still, it is perhaps fitting, at the end of a book which attempts to explain
many of Pope's allusions and help with the background to his poems, to
ask about the necessity for such help and whether it does not make a
response to the poems more rather than less difficult, by intruding
between the reader and the poet.

Specimen question and answer

How necessary is it to understand the historical allusions in Pope's
satires?

Pope's poems are saturated with his own times. Although he was,
politically and religiously, an outsider to his society, and although his
poor health prevented his participating in many activities of life, in his
verse he really does hold up a mirror to nature, reflecting especially the
lives, and vices, of the rich. *The Rape of the Lock*, for instance, is a picture
of a day in the life of a society beauty; it describes in detail her evening
pleasures, cards and coffee. Pope's satires are crammed with references
to the politics and social conduct of the reigns of Queen Anne and the
first Hanoverians.

The new reader of Pope feels that his ignorance of the meaning of
Pope's historical allusions prevents his fully understanding the poems.
He anxiously searches for footnotes to explain to whom Pope refers and
why he does so. Without such information, the new reader feels he has
missed a large part of the poet's meaning.

This is not entirely true, for the detailed references in Pope's poems
serve a more general moral purpose. His criticism of Belinda's trivial
morality in *The Rape of the Lock* is evident enough, and momentous

enough, without our knowing about Arabella Fermor and Lord Petre. His attack on extravagance in the 'Timon's villa' passage of *To Burlington* has universal moral significance, and Timon, like Sir Balaam in *To Bathurst*, is a character not to be identified with any one historical individual. The search for the historical detail behind Pope's references, if it takes us away from attending to his moral message, may in fact divert us from what ought to hold our attention in Pope's works. Stressing the historical aspect of his poems may make it difficult for us to see their relevance to us and our own times.

Part 5

Suggestions for further reading

The text

BUTT, JOHN (ED.): *The Twickenham Edition of the Poems of Alexander Pope,* Methuen, London, Yale University Press, New Haven, Connecticut, six volumes, 1939–54. The standard edition, with full notes and commentaries. Available in a one-volume paperback edition, with reduced notes.

DOBRÉE, BONAMY (ED.): *Alexander Pope: Collected Poems,* Dent, London, 1924. A cheap but unreliable text of most of Pope's works.

BROCKBANK, PHILIP (ED.): *Selected Poems of Pope,* Hutchinson English Texts, London, 1964. The text referred to in these notes.

HEATH-STUBBS, JOHN (ED.): *Selected Poems of Alexander Pope,* Heinemann, London, 1964. Contains many of the poems referred to in these notes.

Critical studies

BROWER, REUBEN A.: *Alexander Pope: the Poetry of Allusion,* Oxford University Press, Oxford, 1959. A study of the classical influences on Pope.

DIXON, PETER: *The World of Pope's Satires,* Methuen, London, 1968. An introduction to the *Epistles* and *Imitations of Horace.*

HUNT, JOHN DIXON (ED.): *Pope: The Rape of the Lock: a Casebook,* Macmillan, London, 1968. A valuable collection of critical studies, from 1714 to 1966.

JACK, IAN: *Augustan Satire,* Oxford University Press, Oxford, 1952. Contains three chapters on Pope.

JOHNSON, SAMUEL: 'Life of Pope' in *Johnson's Lives of the Poets: a Selection,* edited by J. P. Hardy, Oxford University Press, London, 1971. An indispensable study by the foremost English critic of the eighteenth century.

LEAVIS, F. R.: *Revaluation,* Penguin Books, Harmondsworth, 1972. Contains an influential chapter on Pope relating him to seventeenth-century poetry.

MACK, MAYNARD: *The Garden and the City,* University of Toronto Press, Toronto; Oxford University Press, London, 1969. An advanced study of the literary and political background of Pope's later poetry.

ROGERS, PAT: *An Introduction to Pope*, Methuen, London, 1975. A survey of Pope's major poems, always readable, sometimes wayward.

SPARKS, PATRICIA MEYER: *An Argument of Images*, Harvard University Press, Cambridge, Massachusetts, 1971. A study of Pope's imagery, including interesting comparisons with poems by Donne, Dryden, Johnson and Eliot.

Background reading

JARRETT, DEREK: *England in the Age of Hogarth*, Hart-Davis, MacGibbon, London, 1974; in paperback, Granada (Paladin), London, 1976. A detailed picture of the early eighteenth century, not confined to London high society.

ROGERS, PAT (ED.): *The Context of English Literature: The Eighteenth Century*, Methuen, London, 1978. A very uneven collection of essays; the first and last are worthless, but the second is a dense account of the politics of the time and the third a clear summary of religion and philosophy.

TRENCH, CHARLES CHENEVIX: *George II*, Allen Lane, London, 1973. A balanced account of the life and reign of the second Hanoverian monarch.

The author of these notes

Christopher MacLachlan was educated at the University of Edinburgh. He is now a lecturer in English at the University of St Andrews. His other publication is an essay on Dryden.